Expecting Greater

Aligning Our Desires with God's Will

By: Janice Broyles

EXPECTING GREATER
ALIGNING OUR DESIRES WITH GOD'S WILL
BY JANICE BROYLES

Published by Late November Literary
Winston Salem, NC 27107

ISBN (Print): 978-1-7352800-9-7
Copyright 2021 by Janice Broyles
Cover design by Sweet N' Spicy designs
Interior design by Late November Literary

Available in print or online. Visit latenovemberliterary.com or janicebroyles.com

All rights reserved. No part of this publication may be reproduced in any form without written permission of the publisher, except as provided by the U.S. copyright law.

All Scriptures are taken from the Holy Bible, King James Version (Public Domain).

Library of Congress Cataloging-in-Publication data
Broyles, Janice.
Expecting Greater: Aligning Our Desires with God's Will / Janice Broyles 1st ed.

Printed in the United States of America

Contents

Foreword: Pastor John Reading 1

Introduction: Not for the Faint of Heart 5

Part I: God's Expectations for His Children: 17

    God's Expectation #1: To Walk In His Will: 19

    God's Expectation #2: To Seek Him First 31

    God's Expectation #3: A Relationship with Him 43

    God's Expectation #4: To Further the Work of His Kingdom 51

    God's Expectation #5: To Trust His Provision 65

    God's Expectations #6: To Get Us Ready for Eternity 73

Part II: Derailing God's Expectations 81

    Derailment #1: Falling into Fear 83

    Derailment #2: Seeking Our Own Lusts 91

    Derailment #3: Listening to the Enemy/Unwise Counsel 99

    Derailment #4: Making Decisions against His Will 107

    Derailment #5: Giving Up 113

    Derailment #6: Getting Offended 121

    Derailment #7: Blaming Others 129

Part III: Pursuing God's Expectations 135

    Godly Pursuit #1: Tap into His Power 137

    Godly Pursuit #2: Take Time to Grow 149

    Godly Pursuit #3: Take Out the Trash 155

    Godly Pursuit #4: Trust Him 167

    Godly Pursuit #5: Truly Submit 177

    Godly Pursuit #6: Work Hard 185

    Godly Pursuit #7: Give Thanks 195

My Letter to You 201

Dedicated to my sons, Jonathan and Benjamin. Never forget that God's plan for your lives is far greater than your own. Trust Him. Xoxo, Mom

Foreword

When asked what I feel is a crucial element to addressing concerns—for example, marriage—my answer takes no time to consider. Expectations.

Unrealistic expectations. Unmet expectations.

Expectations aren't consciously created but are subtlety developed, shaped, and woven into our existence. Starting in childhood we are told by our beloved, well-worn stories that everything works out happily ever after.

But what about when it doesn't?

Being the youngest sibling and only boy with four older sisters, one of my earliest memories of my sisters' schooling was their time in Home Economics class. Their class project was to create a scrapbook for their expected life. They got to plot out the ideal husband, house, and number of kids.

Taking photos cut from magazines, they built a perfect life. Grand, elegant, carefree, exciting, picture-perfect. I remember one of my sisters and her friends sitting on the floor with magazines all over, sharing and comparing, plotting and dreaming. Somehow the dreamy plans of youthful optimism is very different from reality.

It isn't whether life will deviate from our plans, but rather what will we do when it does? When expectations aren't met?

Expectations aren't wrong, and anticipating good things from life isn't bad. It's when we assume what we have come to expect is the ultimate.

In the example of marriage, blending two lives tends to be harder than we thought. It's more than the mixing of two sets of expectations, but also the expectations of parents, family, and others who have shaped them. Is it any wonder we get married and then ask, "Who is this person?" It's not that they've changed overnight, but all of these expectations moved in with them. I read once that expectations in marriage are assumptions we didn't know we had until they went unmet. If topics such as holidays and how and where to celebrate them, balancing spending versus saving, and even food preparation can cause so much angst, what about topics even more core to our eternal existence?

Janice Broyles takes us on a journey into the realm of expectations. With her particular expertise, she has the skill of gently prying off layers, exposing assumptions, and making it all so simple that it now seems obvious.

Unless we become aware and address the concepts that she

presents, they can derail purpose and frustrate God's plans for our lives. Janice has a gift for making profound things attainable for all audiences. She does this through tremendous writing abilities, and also through her unselfish transparency.

Janice does not hide behind popular thought or borrow someone's theories, but she has lived and learned. As such, we are better for her experiences as she shares the richness of her life in the pages of her books.

~Pastor John Reading
Faith Apostolic Church
Greenfield, Indiana

Expect Greater

> ***For as the heavens are higher than the earth, so are my ways higher than your ways, and my thoughts than your thoughts.***
>
> ***Isaiah 55:9***

Introduction
Not for the Faint of Heart

When I walked across the platform at the University of Michigan's Dearborn campus, I held my head high. As a first-generation college graduate, I was so proud of the accomplishment. I heard my family cheering, and my heart swelled. This was it. This was going to launch me into my destiny. I just knew it.

I had already been interviewing. Since I graduated in December, I hoped to step into a teaching position at the start of the January semester. My husband and I were struggling to pay the bills, and with the new baby, our financial struggles only compounded. With Jonathan, our son, being born premature, he had to stay in the NICU for two weeks, not to mention the extended time I had to stay in the hospital due to preeclampsia. John's meager insurance helped where it could, but needless to say, our bills were staggering to a young family who needed government assistance to pay for the baby's food.

But I knew that God would open the right door. God would honor our faithfulness and would place me in the perfect teaching job. I envisioned myself in a high school classroom, changing minds and nurturing intellectual growth. Yes, I would be the best teacher, and John would finally be able to go back to school and finish his college degree. Jonathan would grow up to be something wildly successful, and our lives would be perfect.

Seven months later after numerous interviews throughout the surrounding area… nothing. Most of them called me back for second and third interviews, but they would select the other finalist. Talk about feeling deflated.

I continued praying.

My prayers seemingly went unanswered.

Our bills kept piling up. I took more babysitting jobs to help in some capacity.

At the end of July, a school district finally offered me a full-time teaching position. The district was over three hours away in Northern Michigan. Over three hours away from family and friends and our church. Still, there was little hesitation, especially when John's job at Coca-Cola easily transferred.

You'd think that would be where my perfect story of walking in God's purpose would continue. As if God Himself wrapped up a lovely gift and put a big, beautiful bow on it and handed it to me. "Here you go, my daughter," He'd say. "Only the best for you." I walked through that open door as a 25-year-old young woman determined to live a contented life, teaching students in a small town.

What I didn't realize in August of 2000 was that I was about to enter some of the darkest wilderness years of my life. It was in this small town where I resided for thirteen years that I would struggle within that school district. I faced rejection and bullying at work while struggling with a worsening health condition caused by stress. John and I watched as Jonathan struggled in school, being labeled with a learning and speech disability. I struggled with second child infertility, only to lose the baby we'd tried for years to conceive halfway through the pregnancy. We took my mother in when she unexpectedly lost her job during the economic crash. Five years later I would find her face-first on the floor beside her bed. The night after her memorial service, I wept bitter tears.

I was angry at God.

I felt defeated.

My story doesn't stop there. That is only one side of the story. It took years for me to see those thirteen years as a blessing. Yes, that's right. A blessing. It was in those thirteen years God worked on me and my family. Am I saying that God used some pretty awful experiences to change me for the better?

That's exactly what I'm saying.

Why would He do that? Why would He allow obstacles, challenges, and heartaches to attack and overwhelm us?

The answer: *expectations*. His versus ours. Spirit versus flesh. Holiness versus carnality. Selflessness versus self-selfishness. Perfect versus flawed.

Let me explain. There is a certain order to life and its circumstances that we come to expect. We expect that if we work 40 hours in a week, we will get paid for our labor. We expect that if we exercise and eat right, our health will improve. We expect that when we get married and say "I do," that we will be with our spouse until death parts us.

Even in smaller ways, we have expectations. We expect that when we prefill the coffee reservoir and set the timer on the coffee pot, we will have hot coffee the next morning. We expect when we go to pump gas, the equipment will work and our car will be full. Sometimes we don't even think about these expectations. We just know.

The challenge is when something happens that breaks the cycle of meeting those expectations. A credit card gets declined, or the coffee pot stops working, or there are layoffs at work, or a spouse makes the decision to end the marriage.

Expectations…not met.

For me, it was agonizing when my expectations of securing a teaching job didn't happen as fast as I wanted. When I stepped into a teaching job and felt so isolated and attacked, I found myself questioning my dreams. Maybe I wasn't supposed to be a teacher? Maybe we never should have moved up north? Maybe God was punishing me?

It never occurred to me that God might have placed me exactly where I needed to be, so He could work on me. The thought never ran through my mind that in my isolation and loneliness I would lean more on Him. And I never thought I actually needed more training on how to be an effective teacher. I also never thought that the criticism helped chisel away at the rough edges of my early teaching career. Maybe if I hadn't been so focused on myself, I would have noticed the incredible people God placed in my life to help me hone my skills. My pride and unwillingness to admit shortcomings hindered me from seeing God's hand.

Hindsight is often 20/20, but I decided once I moved from that town and into another teaching position somewhere else that I wouldn't let my past struggles tag along. I would do better and be better. I would open myself up to God's direction and sometimes gentle rebukes.

As I continue to journey through life, I've learned that in

my humble submission, God can finally take the reins that I've stubbornly held onto. I've realized that I, many times, sabotaged His will. He had expectations for me that surpassed anything I could imagine, but those expectations would never be realized without me stepping away from the façade of control I thought I had on my life.

This is a fine line and one that can be frustrating. How do I merge my expectations for my life with God's? How do I align my desires with His? How do I let go of what I want and trust that He knows best?

If we're honest with ourselves, we can admit that unrealized expectations have the potential to lead to a host of negative outcomes. From frustration and inconvenience to rejection, betrayal, and bitterness, multiple levels of disappointment can impact us, depending on the severity of the setback.

Expectations Defined

We have expectations in every single area of our lives. And the same is true in our walk with God. To expect something is *to anticipate* its occurrence. Another definition is to have *an assurance* that what's expected will happen. With God, faith and expectations go together, but sometimes we don't consider that God has expectations for us, especially when we choose to walk in a relationship with Him. Do you have expectations for your spouse or significant other? Of course! And since we are the bride of Christ, expectations go both ways in the relationship.

He believes in us. That's what it means when we consider that God has a purpose, a specific plan, for our lives. In

Jeremiah 1:5, God says, "Before I formed thee in the belly, I knew thee; and before thou camest forth out of the womb I sanctified thee, and I ordained thee a prophet unto the nations." So, not only does He know us before we were born, but He also has *expectations* for each of us. He has an anticipated future for us, but we must be willing participants for that future to be realized.

Some may question why God would have expectations for us. He already knows we fall short. He sent His Son to save the world because we could never be justified and cleansed otherwise. However, when we choose Christ, not only are we His bride, but we are adopted into Him. We are the royal priesthood. Do you not think there are expectations as we step into this heavenly covenant? Did not God expect Moses, Joshua, Samuel, and Samson—along with many others—to keep His commandments? The Word says, "Be ye holy, for I am holy," (I Peter 1:16). That's an expectation. If we are to follow Him, He *expects* us to be like Him.

God's Purpose, Plans, & Expectations

The terms "purpose," "plans," and "expectations" are often used synonymously, and I fall into this writing conundrum myself. However, each holds slight variations of meaning. Purpose is defined as the reason something is done. Plans refer to an intention about what one is going to do, which makes the term more specific. Expectations are the anticipation that something is going to happen.

Think of it this way: He has a *purpose* for our lives that involves His *plans* being fulfilled. He *expects* us to do our part in realizing those plans.

Here's what we need to understand:
1. We are not an accident or a mistake. God knows us, and He loves us. If we are here on earth, we are here for a reason. This is *purpose*.
2. God has greater *plans* for us than we have for ourselves. But He *expects* us to walk in His will for these plans to come to fruition.
3. His *plans* are higher than ours. His *expectations* for us are for our good and betterment.
4. These *expectations* are not to fulfill our selfish desires but to prepare us to walk in His *purpose* (which is service to His kingdom).
5. Without a servant's heart and willingness to obey, God's *expectations* of His fulfilled *purpose* for our lives will never be realized.
6. It is because He loves you that He wants you to be the BEST you can be, and that starts with working on your inward man.
7. Whether or not God's *expectations* for our lives are ever realized is dependent upon us.

Consider Joseph. He had a dream. To get to the fulfillment of that dream, he endured rejection by his brothers. He was sold into slavery, convicted of a crime he didn't commit, thrown into a dungeon to rot, and forgotten by someone he helped. Yet through those experiences, God worked on Joseph's character. Ultimately, Joseph rose to power in Egypt, saving his family from drought and famine. But the journey to that point was years of mistreatment and anguish.

Consider David. He had a promise. The journey to that promise consisted of multiple rejections: one from his father and the other from a father-figure, King Saul. He was also rejected by his brothers and rejected by his best friend and brother-in-arms, Prince Jonathan. He was forced to live on the run for years, forced to live within the enemy's camp, and forced himself not to retaliate against the king who wanted him dead. If that wasn't bad enough, he had to watch his bride be handed over to another man. Through all of that, he became king and led Judah and Israel to victory on several occasions, and the Bible says that he was a man after God's heart.

Consider Moses. From the very beginning of his life, he had to hide (his identity and then his whereabouts). Even when he tried to help his people, he was rejected by them. He was also rejected by his brother (Pharaoh). For years he led the children of Israel, helping them break free from Pharaoh's iron grip and leading them to their promised land. But the journey was anything but easy.

Consider Mary. She was told by an angel that she was blessed and highly favored. Then she was given a promise. This led to initial rejection by her betrothed and by her people. She was then forced to hide and give birth in a barn and forced to flee the country and live in a foreign place (Egypt) for years. Most importantly, she had to watch her son be ridiculed and mercilessly killed. Yet she was one of the 120 in the upper room who received the Holy Spirit in Acts chapter two.

Comfort versus Commitment

Have the warm fuzzies yet? All of these examples show similar concepts. God's plans involved expectations for them, but none of it was easy. Not one iota of it. Every scenario required the individuals to submit, trust, and work. Yet God's ultimate plan was blessing and provision for them *and* those around them. That doesn't mean God kept them in comfortable situations.

Wait a sec, so God's plans don't involve giving me millions of dollars, a nice car, and a fancy condo in Florida? The simple answer: that's not too high on God's priority list. He will give us the resources needed for accomplishing His will. The Bible says that He provides and that He also wants to give us the desires of our hearts. The Bible even says that we don't get what we pray for because we pray with the wrong motive. God examines the heart, and ultimately, He's not too concerned with our comfort. When we're too comfortable, our relationship with God may be placed on the backburner.

What if I told you that God isn't as concerned about your comfort as He is with your commitment? What if I told you that money in your bank account means nothing to Him in comparison to the content of your character? And that His will for your life may be the most frustrating, challenging experience you will ever face, yet it is perfect, kind, and meant for your ultimate good and divine destiny?

Many of us tend to see God as this omniscient, omnipotent being outside of time that observes from afar. When I was young, I listened to my Sunday School teachers talk about this great, mighty, all-powerful Lord. I envisioned some old man with a long beard and piercing eyes, staring at everything with a deep frown. I found the concept fascinating, albeit largely intimidating.

In my imagination, I could see Him forming the universe and speaking things into existence. But when it got to the part of this same God walking around the Garden of Eden with

Adam and Eve, my child's brain was like, "Say what? This great big God walked next to Adam?" I tried to envision this old, bearded man with the deep frown walking around with some guy, and I found it absurd. Wasn't God as tall as a building? How'd that work? And if it worked for Adam, how come God never came and took a walk with me?

I remember when I first heard the story of Moses up on Mount Sinai talking with God. He wanted to see God's face, but God told him that couldn't happen because it'd kill him. Then God came up with a plan to place Moses in the cleft of the rock, that way God could pass by and Moses could see a glimpse of Him passing by. I thought that was incredible! But what made Moses so special? And could I be special like him?

Later in my life, I began to understand something very profound: all of these examples show how much God desires a relationship with His people. He is not some old guy with a long white beard and a deep frown. He's personable and desires intimacy with His creation. Part of intimacy and relationship is *expectation*. Just as we expect certain things from our spouse, God has certain expectations for us. He *expects* us to trust Him. He *expects* us to love Him and to let Him into our lives. He also *expects* questions and communication too, but not at the expense of trust.

Final Thoughts

We have expectations for God. We stand upon the Word that He is faithful to be with us and lead us in the correct path. But expecting greater is understanding that God has expectations for us as well. He expects us to do our part in the fulfillment of His plans for our lives. Many of us are probably glad to hear it. Some of us may wish that He would clarify a few things. Scripture does provide very specific clarifications of God-ordained expectations:

- They are perfect.
- They are imparted through the Holy Scripture.
- They are for our good.
- They are specific to each of us and our talents.
- They will require us to step outside our comfort zone.
- They will require our submission.
- They will require our obedience.
- They will require service.

If you are struggling in your walk with God, trying to figure out His will, trying to grapple with things that don't make sense and are not convenient, or if you are struggling with disappointment, feeling as if you have done everything right, but circumstances are not turning out the way you need them to, then take heart. God is not upset over your questions or frustration. He is sovereign, and He is not intimidated by our humanity. On the contrary, He has greater expectations for our lives than we have for ourselves, and He patiently waits for us to come to Him. If we give Him the reins and let Him take control, the journey will not be without reward.

As you read through this book, you'll see it's divided into three sections. The first section discusses God's expectations for our lives. They are outlined in Scripture, and we'll walk through what they are and what they mean for us. The second section of the book looks at different ways we sabotage God's will and His expectations for our lives. This is important in understanding why God's plan can sometimes be derailed (Hint: it's not Him, it's us). The third section walks us through how to live within the purpose of God to experience all He has for us.

Part I:
God's Expectations for His Children

> *Not everyone that saith unto me, Lord, Lord, shall enter the kingdom of heaven, but he that doeth the will of my Father which is in heaven.*
> *~Matthew 7:21*

God's Expectation #1: To Walk In His Will

The message had been simple: don't touch the soup. My mother stood over the stove, stirring the large pot of homemade chicken noodle soup, and I wanted some. As she ladled some into several bowls, she looked at me pointedly. "Don't touch the soup, Janice. It's hot. You'll burn yourself."

She set the bowls on the table, the steam rising from them. The temptation was too much. I walked over to them only to look. I might have been around five or six, but I understood what hot meant. There was a part of me that was curious about how hot they were. I remember checking to see that Mom's attention was elsewhere before I lifted my finger to the bowl. My objective was to put my finger in the bowl to see if what Mom said was true.

And she had told the truth. The soup scalded my finger, so I pulled it back away from the bowl. Unfortunately, my finger caught the edge of the bowl, and in a split second, the bowl dumped its contents all down my little shirt and onto my chest.

I screamed and thankfully Mom moved quickly. I ended up having first degree burns, and I learned a valuable lesson.

When it comes to our walk with God, we often question His will. Sometimes we know not to do something (because the Bible specifically tells us not to), but the temptation is too much. We go against what we were told *not* to do. It might be just a little diversion off the divine path, just like my finger in the soup, but testing the waters of something outside of God's will can easily result in a flood of consequences that He never intended for us.

Let's be real. Most of us don't enjoy being told what to do. We may struggle with those in leadership positions over us. We don't like reprimands or criticism. We feel that we have the answers, and even if we don't, we feel that we can figure it out for ourselves. This amazing gift God gave us back in the very beginning has been mismanaged and abused to the point of being our detriment and sometimes leading to our ruin.

Free will.

In the whole of creation, we were special. Made in God's image. God purposefully set us aside, designed by His very hand. You see, all of creation worships Him. The trees, the plants and flowers, even the rocks will cry out when the time comes. But He desired more than just commanded reverence. He wanted relationship. In a relationship, love is mutually shared. There is no coercion. True love encompasses both. For this relationship to work with mankind, we were given free will. How much more beautiful it would be if we would choose Him and love Him!

Unfortunately for us, free will comes down to choices, and we don't have the greatest track record of wise decisions. Adam and Eve started that not-too-proud tradition for humanity. God placed them in paradise and told them that it was all theirs. They would walk with Him and talk with Him. God's expectations to nourish and grow that relationship came to a catastrophic halt when Eve's decision sabotaged destiny.

Adam's decision to take part in Eve's mistake severed the intimate relationship with God. On that fateful day, sin entered the garden. Since sin cannot be where God is, Adam and Eve had to leave. Cast out and cursed, their act of free will affected the rest of humanity for generations upon generations.

Free will gives us the power to do what we want. Therefore, our expectations depend upon the choices we make, along with the decisions of others. That's right. Other people's decisions and acts of free will affect your expectations as well. You may have worked hard for the promotion, but your manager chooses someone else. Expectations thwarted thanks to someone else's decision.

Unfortunately, the enemy has taken the gift of free will in our lives and perverted it to fit his agenda. One only needs to turn on the news to see the enemy at work. His agenda is anger, divisiveness, conflict, abuse, murder, and on and on. People's decisions often cost them dearly, and to make it worse, negatively affect others around them. This perpetual cycle only furthers the dysfunction.

Take a look at the sexual revolution that began in the 1960s. The idea of rejecting traditional roles, including the rejection of monogamous relationships within marriages, took off like a wildfire. Men and women wanted to break free from what was mostly an inaccurate perception of a boring, dull life with only one partner. God's will of marriage between one man and one woman until death do us part became antiquated and repressive. The results were both direct and indirect:

- An increase in sexually transmitted diseases (STDs). There are over 20 STDs, and several of them have no cure.
- The legalization of abortion. Millions of unborn lives

have been taken since Roe v. Wade in 1973.
- More and more people are deciding to put off marriage. Many are choosing to not get married at all.
- More unwed mothers raising children by themselves.
- Children in one-parent homes being raised in poverty. This leads to more poverty.
- Those in poverty often break the law. Their desperation pushes them to make bad decisions. Those bad decisions lead to hurting themselves or hurting others. Their actions then lead to a life behind bars. The majority of prisoners come from a life of poverty.

All of these situations probably existed long before the sexual revolution, but they were definitely magnified and expanded because of it.

The concept of "No one tells me what to do" has also increased throughout our culture over the last several decades, and it has wreaked havoc on the church. Born-again believers openly live in sin, refusing to repent because their sin is justified in their own eyes. Church leaders become misguided by the concept of a loving, accepting Jesus, so much so that they look away from blatant sins, afraid that they'll be considered judgmental or hypocritical. When our stubbornness and lack of repentance are applied to our personal relationship with God, we take Him off the throne of our hearts—if He was ever there, to begin with—and place ourselves there instead.

The Bible says that God is jealous in the sense that He will not come second to another. It's not going to happen. At the same time, God is a gentleman and allows us to walk our own paths. He doesn't force us to do His will. There is no bribing or manipulating. Just like with Adam and Eve, God gave us free will because ultimately, the choice is ours.

We either want Him in our lives, or we don't.

We either want His will, or we want to make our own decisions and be in control of our own destinies.

But as Jesus warned in Matthew, no one can serve two masters. That right there is a powerful nugget of truth: We are serving one master or the other. When we make our own choices, we have chosen our flesh as the master of our lives.

And any time we listen to our flesh, there are selfish motives behind it. Every. Single. Time.

So, what is God's will? How do I know if I'm walking in it? Those are good questions.

- *It is God's will for every person to be saved.*
  "For this is good and acceptable in the sight of God our Savior; who will have all men to be saved, and to come unto the knowledge of truth," (I Timothy 2:3-4).
- *It is God's will for us to be thankful in everything.*
  "In everything give thanks: for this is the will of God in Christ concerning you," (I Thessalonians 5:18).
- *It is God's will for us to be sanctified and to abstain from sexual immorality.*
  "For this is the will of God, [even] your sanctification, that ye should abstain from fornication," (I Thessalonians 4:3).
- *It is God's will for us to deny our flesh, which means casting aside selfishness and hedonistic pleasures.*
  "And [Jesus] said to them all, 'If any man will come after me, let him deny himself, and take up his cross daily, and follow me,'" (Luke 9:23).
- *It is God's will for us to behave upright at all times to*

silence doubters.
"For so is the will of God, that with well doing ye may put to silence the ignorance of foolish men," (I Peter 2:15).

- ***It is God's will for us to be filled with the Holy Spirit.***
"Wherefore be ye not unwise, but understanding what the will of the Lord is. And be not drunk with wine, wherein is excess; but be filled with the Spirit; Speaking to yourselves in psalms and hymns and spiritual songs, singing and making melody in your heart to the Lord; Giving thanks always for all things unto God…" (Ephesians 5:17-20).

- ***It is God's will for all to repent and turn to Him.***
"The Lord is not slack concerning his promise…but is longsuffering to us-ward, not willing that any should perish, but that all should come to repentance," (2 Peter 3:9).

- ***It is God's will for us to be merciful, just, and humble.***
"…And what doth the Lord require of thee, but to do justly, and to love mercy, and to walk humbly with thy God," (Micah 6:8).

- ***It is God's will for us to seek Him and His kingdom first.***
"But seek ye first the kingdom of God, and his righteousness; and all these things shall be added unto you," (Matthew 6:33).

From these verses, it is evident that God's will involves seeking Him first, salvation, sanctification, denying one's flesh, sexual purity, being thankful, being humble and merciful, being filled with the Spirit, living a life of worship before Him, and doing good so that critics are silenced. This is a tall order, but He wouldn't ask it of us if it was impossible.

Noah

There are many times when we feel as if God does not make any sense. Noah was probably no exception. He was an upright man who feared and honored God. That alone saved his life and the lives of his family, but that favor led to quite an adventure.

> *And God looked upon the earth, and, behold, it was corrupt... And God said unto Noah, The end of all flesh is come before me... I will destroy them with the earth. Make thee an ark of gopher wood; rooms shalt thou make in the ark, and shalt pitch it within and without with pitch...But with thee will I establish my covenant; and thou shalt come into the ark, thou, and thy sons, and thy wife, and thy sons' wives with thee. Genesis 6:12-14,18 (condensed)*

To save his life and the lives of his family and all the species of animals, he had to be obedient.

Think about that initial conversation. The God of the universe tells you that (1) He's going to destroy all flesh because of how wicked everyone is, (2) He's going to do so by flooding the earth, (3) To survive, Noah is going to have to build an ark that will house Noah and his family, along with a set of animals from every species, and (4) God is going to establish a covenant with Noah and use his seed to continue the human race.

How many of us would have a few questions?

For roughly 100 years, Noah had to follow God's plan and build a gigantic structure. Do you wonder if at some point within those 100 years that Noah doubted? Many of us have been called by God, yet we question Him within weeks or months! However, Noah did what was asked of him, even when it did not make sense, and even when others questioned him. Following God's plan, ultimately protected him and his family and continued the human race.

Abraham

How would you handle the situation if God told you to move? Pack up what you can and head out, and God will tell you where to go and when to stop. Try telling your spouse, "Hey babe, we're moving. When? Right now. Just grab what you can and let's go. Why? Because God told me to." When God called Abram, that's about what happened.

> *Now the Lord had said unto Abram, Get thee out of thy country, and from thy kindred, and from thy father's house, unto a land that I will shew thee: And I will make of thee a great nation, and I will bless thee, and make thy name great; and thou shalt be a blessing...*
> *Genesis 12:1-2*

God had a plan. He set aside a people that would be His. It would be through this lineage that His plan for mankind's redemption would take place, but first He needed a willing vessel. Someone who would do His will. We don't know if God tried other men first. All we know is that Abraham obeyed. God's will for Abraham's life far exceeded anything that the man could concoct on his own. With Abraham's obedience to God's will came protection and prosperity. More than that, there was a relationship. Abraham was considered a friend of God.

There was one aspect of God's promise that troubled Abraham: a promised child. At the time, Abram and Sarai desired a son. God's plan would do more than just give him a son, it would produce a great nation, but that didn't make sense to Abraham and Sarah. They were old. How could that be possible?

There was a point in their relationship with God that Abraham and Sarah questioned God's will. God had promised them a son, and even more than that, God promised that Abraham would be the "father of many nations." Sounds great. Then the years started passing by. Abraham and Sarah started to question His will. Sarah told her husband, "Maybe God meant for you to have a son through my handmaiden."

There it was. Doubt.

Abraham ended up marrying Hagar, Sarah's servant, and she gave birth to Ishmael. What resulted were complications. Lots of them. Sarah became extremely jealous. Hagar started provoking her former master. Sarah abused her to the point that Hagar ran away. Abraham was caught in the middle. Eventually, when 90-year-old Sarah gave birth to Isaac, the tension between the two brothers grew to the point that Hagar and her son were forced to leave. All of this a result of making the wrong choice, letting doubt sabotage God's plan, and stepping outside His will.

Even with their wrong choices, God still accomplished His will, and Isaac was born. Unfortunately, a lot of conflict and frustration resulted due to stepping away from God's plan. The conflict between these two brothers is still felt today.

Final Thoughts

The message may sound simple: God has expectations for each of us, a plan for our lives, but He leaves it to us to make the choice. His way or ours. The follow-through is a challenge because for God's expectations to reach fulfillment, He is counting on us to walk in His will. This is a deliberate choice on our part.

Oftentimes, His will looks different than our own, which means we need to surrender our will to His. Many of us struggle to do this:

- We don't mind serving Him, but it's got to be on our terms.
- We don't mind answering His call, as long as it doesn't jeopardize our comfort.
- We'll be ministry-minded if we see quick results and receive continued accolades.

This flawed way of thinking does not mesh with an infinite God. If our version of Christianity is on our terms, then we are not truly serving Him. If we refuse to sacrifice for the sake of His will, then we are like the rich, young ruler turning away from Jesus' ministry (more on this later).

The truth is that God's will is not easy. Choosing to serve Him completely means dying to our flesh. Paul said in 1 Corinthians that he died to his flesh daily. In my own life, I've learned:

- God's will is not always meant to be understood. It's meant to be trusted.
- God's will does not need our direction or advice.
- God's will is for His glory, not ours.
- God's will is far better than our own.

When I finally stopped fighting God, I found His perfect peace. I've discovered that His will may not take me down life's least complicated road, but His will protects and prospers me, even in the midst of a storm.

> *...Know ye not that the friendship of the world is enmity with God? whosoever therefore will be a friend of the world is the enemy of God...Submit yourselves therefore to God. Resist the devil, and he will flee from you.*
>
> *James 4:4, 7*

God's Expectation #2: To Seek Him First

About six years ago, I nearly gave up writing. I had just read my 200th rejection, and something inside me snapped. I remember pushing myself away from my desk, standing up, and saying out loud, "That's it. I'm done."

At the time, I was writing children's books and young adult fiction. I had five completed novels that I aggressively queried. All of the novels were good. They had been critiqued by my critique group. They had been read through by agents and editors. They had been revised and rewritten several times over. I had accomplished some modicum of success. I secured a literary agent who loved my work and was determined to help me sell it. Once I signed on the dotted line, I knew that this was it. I would be signed by a major publisher, and I would become a successful author.

But that didn't happen.

Around the time I walked away from my desk, determining to be done with writing forever, I took a trip to Florida to visit my sister. I was not in a good place emotionally, spiritually, or professionally. My mother had only recently passed away, my family and I had sold our house and were trying to make it in my uncle's cabin until some door opened for us, and I was miserable at my teaching job, dreading the thought of returning in the fall. Visiting my sister was just the escape I needed.

My sister and I were in the car when we got on the topic of my writing. I was quickly becoming annoyed because I didn't feel like listening to advice, especially from someone who had never written a book. Then she said the words that eventually changed everything: "Have you asked God what He wants you to write?"

"Yes, I have," I said, a little too sharply, even though I knew I hadn't. In the nearly ten years I had actively pursued a writing career, had I ever asked God for direction? I warred within myself. Surely, I had asked Him. Most of my prayer time focused on my writing, but the more I thought about it, the more I realized that my prayers were mostly begging God to open the doors for success. My version of success, not necessarily His.

Not long after that Florida trip, I grudgingly asked God for His direction. "Okay, God, what do you want me to write?" I still thought it was silly. Why would God care what I wrote?

Months later, the idea came suddenly. I can't even pinpoint where it came from, but I kept feeling pushed to write a story about David. I ignored it for nearly a year. I wasn't about to write a story about a Bible character. The Bible already did a great job. Besides, do you know how much research and study would go into something like that? No way. Not my thing.

The push was so strong that I finally threw up my hands. I remember sitting down at the computer months after my decision to give up, telling myself to just write a chapter. I didn't feel confident in it at all. Still, I began to research and really study the books in the Old Testament that chronicled his story. "I'm not good enough to tell his story," I'd say in my prayer time.

My friend invited me to a fall writer's conference. I'd already attended about a dozen within ten years and felt discouraged about spending the money. But this conference was different. It was a Christian writer's conference. I thought of my David book. Maybe I could get some insight there. I told my friend that I would apply for the scholarship. If I was approved, then I could go.

I was granted the scholarship, so I decided to walk through the open door and get help for my David chapters.

The night before we were leaving for the conference, I realized I had signed up for a nonfiction proposal workshop. The David book was a fictional retelling, so I couldn't use that in the session.

I wanted to learn more about nonfiction writing, but I hadn't realized I needed to bring sample writing with me. When I glanced at the email directions, it said to have a nonfiction proposal. I didn't have one! All I had were a couple of chapters done of the David story. Feeling rushed, I threw something together. I didn't even really think about it. I just took a topic that God had been working with me on and wrote up some notes and a table of contents.

The nonfiction workshop was the first session of the conference. I explained to the instructor that my proposal was rough because I had never written a nonfiction proposal before. She asked to read through it to provide some feedback. When she was done, she looked up and said, "This is powerful. I can see this getting published."

My mouth must have hung open! I was floored. But that wasn't it. During the entire conference, several editors and writing professionals read through my notes, and they said the same thing. "This needs to be published."

Ironically, there wasn't much interest in the David story, at least, not yet.

When I got home after the conference, I read and reread all the notes on my nonfiction proposal. I shook my head in disbelief. "Do you really want me to write about this?" I asked God. The topic would reopen a lot of old wounds. I would have to write about my past, about my mother's death. I knew that God wouldn't have allowed me to go to that conference and have all those business professionals tell me the same thing. I prayed, "If you want me to write this book, I need your strength."

Two months later, I had secured a traditional publisher for my book, *No Longer Rejected: A Woman's Journey from Rejection to Freedom.*

The following year, I went back to that same Christian conference. It was there I met an editor who showed interest in my recently finished novel about David, *The Secret Heir.* Four months later, I had signed a contract for that book with that publisher.

It took thirteen years from the start of my writing journey to see my first book in print.

What would have happened if I had sought God first from the very beginning?

Even now, I have surrendered complete control of my dream to the Lord, but I have to arm-wrestle my flesh into submission, which is hard to do. Very hard.

The Children of Israel

According to Scripture, God expects us to seek Him first. Just as I stated in chapter one, He refuses to be in second place. When He is not first, we subject ourselves to faulty decisions, unwise counsel (which includes listening to ourselves), and extenuating difficulties.

And the Lord's anger was kindled against Israel, and he made them wander in the wilderness forty years, until all the generation, that had done evil in the sight of the Lord, was consumed.
Numbers 32:13

The children of Israel struggled to keep God first, despite His deliverance and protection. Their negativity and refusal to believe that God would keep His promises kindled God's anger. He had them wander around the wilderness for forty years. Not only that but because of their unwillingness to put Him first and follow His commandments, only two from that entire generation stepped into the promised land. God's expectations hadn't changed, but the children of Israel were volatile, double-minded, and full of complaints. They had a hard time keeping Egypt back where it belonged.

The first commandment God gave them was simple: He came first. Nothing else came before Him. Yet while God had this conversation with Moses on Mount Sinai, the children of Israel were erecting a golden calf. I don't want to point a finger at these people because I know many times I have become impatient waiting on God. How many times have I taken matters into my own hands? I might not erect a golden cow in my living room, but how many times have I esteemed other people's opinions above God's direction? How many times have I valued my desires more than His Word?

We've already discussed in the previous chapter walking in His will. That cannot happen when we do not seek Him first. Seeking Him means that we esteem Him and His ways above all else. These two expectations, therefore, go together.

Take a look at certain situations that are frustrating to you right now.
- Work or career-related issues?
- Family-related issues?
- Financial issues?
- Procrastination issues?
- Health issues?

Now ask yourself if you have taken these frustrations to the Lord first. Before you've discussed it with friends or significant others, have you prayed about it? If you find yourself hesitating here, you are not alone. Here are some of the excuses I've used in my own life situations:
- *This is just a little thing.*
- *I can handle this.*
- *I don't need to pray about every small problem that presents itself.*
- *I need to talk to someone who will actually give me advice.*
- *I will pray about it, but I need to make a decision now.*
- *God doesn't want to hear about all my problems.*
- *There are bigger issues in the world.*

- *I shouldn't be so selfish praying about every little thing.*
- *I can't take every moment of every day and pray about everything. Who has time for that?*

If any of these thoughts—or variations of them—have crossed your mind at some point, welcome to the club. The challenge is that these are all excuses that ultimately remove God from being first in our lives. What if we said these statements instead?

- *If God knows about every sparrow that falls, nothing is too little for Him to know about or to help with. He knows it all, yet He waits for us to ask for help.*
- *I can do all things…THROUGH CHRIST…that means that the only way I can truly handle anything is through Him.*
- *The Bible says to cast my cares on Him. It doesn't say what size those cares have to be.*
- *His Word is His advice. What does the Bible say about my situation?*
- *I always have time to ask God to direct my steps. I don't want to make any decision without first asking God to lead the way.*
- *Having a daily walk with God means that God is always by my side.*
- *He's as close as the mention of His name. It doesn't get any more convenient than that!*

Let me clarify that I'm not necessarily talking about praying over every little decision, such as where to go for lunch. When we are living a life in total surrender to Jesus, He is already directing our steps. In our time with Him, whether it's our morning devotion or just a simple prayer we pray on the way to work, taking the time to acknowledge Him and His ways will lead to His guidance throughout the day.

When I think back to the children of Israel in Exodus 32, and their erecting of a golden calf, I am bothered that Aaron, Moses' brother, listened to the crowd. Surely, he knew that building an idol wasn't the best idea. Yet the Bible says that "the people gathered themselves together unto Aaron." How long did he listen to their demands? How long did it take before he finally gave in? In this instance, he listened to the voices around him instead of seeking God amid the chaos.

The enemy knows that we get ourselves in trouble when we don't seek God above all else. He uses several tactics to make sure we don't seek God first.

1. **Distractions**

    This has become a major challenge in the 21st century. We have a variety of products and people vying for our attention. Even now, while typing this, my cell phone rests beside me, buzzing periodically. I pause, then look to see who is trying to reach me. During my prayer time, I am often distracted. I try to have my cell phone in a completely separate room. Sometimes, I'll be praying only to have someone in my household interrupt me, or my thoughts start to drift in different directions. If I'm not careful, these distractions can pull me away from a deeper walk with God.

2. **Busyness**

   We are distracted because we are busy. We are busy with our families, busy with our churches, busy with careers. Busy, busy, busy. We have to be diligent to prevent the enemy from using our busyness as a stumbling block. If we are too busy to pray and seek God first, then we are *too* busy. We need to prioritize and get our 'spiritual' house in order so that God is not forgotten in our day-to-day lives.

3. **Our need for approval**

   When we seek others' opinions before God's will, we set ourselves up for struggle. Our need for approval forces us to look toward others for accolades and acceptance. It doesn't necessarily feel good to stand out. The enemy uses that as leverage against us. We then make hasty and, at times, unwise decisions just to fit in.

4. **Offense**

   It is hard to put God first when our hearts are not right. Being offended has turned people's hearts away from God since before the rich young ruler of Mark 10. Our relationship with God is personal, and other people should not sway or divide that relationship, but that is exactly what happens when we become hurt or upset. We, if not careful, transfer that hurt toward God.

5. **Impatience**

   This is a common culprit for hasty decisions, and it has gotten many people into complicated situations simply because they refused to wait. With this tactic, we don't want to wait on God's timing, or we rationalize that we will help Him out by making a quick decision. Sarah's impatience in bearing a son created conflict within their family unit and ultimately created conflict between two nations of people. Don't let impatience create ripples in your life that will affect generations to come.

6. **Materialism**

We live in a hedonistic society where materialism reigns supreme. If you want it, go get it. There are payment plans, credit cards, and bank loans to help you get it faster and easier than ever. We are so busy buying the newest "must-have," that we ignore the Bible's admonition to not go into debt because we become slaves to the lender (Proverbs 22:7). Once we have what we want, we often lose interest, yet we're stuck with the debt or stuck with items that clutter the house unused. Then we set our sights on the next "must-have," not realizing that God is nowhere in the equation. The enemy's strategy with materialism is to distract us with things, which ultimately leads us away from the presence of God.

7. **Covetousness**

Part of the sin of materialism comes from coveting what others have. My youngest son, who is twelve at the time of this writing, wants a cell phone because his friends have cell phones. It's a source of contention at times with Benjamin, but my husband and I explain to him that we are not other kids' parents. We are *his* parents, and we believe that preteens should not have cell phones. This strategy from the enemy places our focus on what other people have. Doing so leads to ungratefulness, jealousy, and possibly depression and anger.

Final Thoughts

God's expectations for our lives will never come to fruition if He is not first. Yet life is full of distractions that keep us focused on other things. Our selfish desires can get in the way of putting Him first in our lives. The only way for this to happen is for us to set aside the distractions, busyness, and sinful desires of our lives and seek Him above all else. As it says in the book of Hebrews: "…let us lay aside every weight, and the sin which doth so easily beset us, and let us run with patience the race that is set before us, looking unto Jesus the author and finisher of our faith…" (Hebrews 12:1-2).

If we want God's plans to be fulfilled in our lives, seeking Him first, above all else, needs to be an integral part of our relationship with Him. He *expects* it of us.

> *The Lord hath appeared of old unto me, saying, Yea, I have loved thee with an everlasting love: therefore with lovingkindness have I drawn thee.*
>
> *Jeremiah 31:3*

God's Expectation #3: A Relationship with Him

Marriage is hard. Two people from different backgrounds come together, decide to cleave to each other, and build a new family. What could go wrong with that?

I met John, my husband, through his grandparents, years before we began dating. He was a backwoods, North Carolina boy, and I was a city-slicker, thriving within the suburbs of the Detroit area. John and his dad would come up to Michigan nearly every year to visit his grandparents and their extended family. Since my family went to the same church as John's grandparents, he would periodically visit our church.

Make no mistake, we were not sweethearts or anything cute or romantic, at least at first. I thought he was a nerd. When I was around the age of thirteen or fourteen, his grandfather told me—in front of my friends, mind you—that little Johnny and I should get married someday. I wanted to crawl under a church pew. I was mortified.

A few years later, John came to live with his grandmother for the summer. Time changes things. He had grown up, as had I. It would be another year or two before we'd start dating and eventually marry.

Cute story. But that was the easy part.

Expect Greater

Even with our common Christian backgrounds, we were very different. Our personalities were different, our outlook on the future was different, how we were raised was *very* different, and what we expected from each other differed as well.

That first year of marriage—man, oh man—was rather tumultuous. What started as two lovebirds with stars in their eyes quickly shifted to reality: two young adults in their early 20s trying to figure out adult life…together.

Despite these differences, our love and friendship flourished. We learned to communicate, trust each other, and rely on one another, but it didn't just happen. It took work. It still takes work.

Samuel

> *…the Lord called Samuel: and he answered, Here am I. And he ran unto Eli, and said, Here am I; for thou calledst me. And he said, I called not; lie down again. And he went and lay down.*
> *And the Lord called yet again, Samuel. And Samuel arose and went to Eli, and said, Here am I; for thou didst call me. And he answered, I called not, my son; lie down again.*
> *Now Samuel did not yet know the Lord, neither was the word of the Lord yet revealed unto him.*
> *And the Lord called Samuel again the third time. And he arose and went to Eli, and said,*

> *Here am I; for thou didst call me. And Eli perceived that the Lord had called the child. Therefore Eli said unto Samuel, Go, lie down: and it shall be, if he call thee, that thou shalt say, Speak, Lord; for thy servant heareth. So Samuel went and lay down in his place.*
>
> *And the Lord came, and stood, and called as at other times, Samuel, Samuel. Then Samuel answered, Speak; for thy servant heareth.*
>
> *1 Samuel 3:4-10*

This account in 1 Samuel illustrates God's desire to be in a relationship with us. Samuel was a young man when this calling occurred. According to this Scripture, he did not yet know the Lord. His mother had honored her promise to God when He provided her a son, and so Samuel was being raised under the mentorship of Eli.

God had a plan for Samuel's life. He needed him to be a prophet to a new generation of kings. Samuel had a calling to fulfill. He could have rolled over and gone back to sleep. He could have outright ignored the Lord's voice. Because he answered the call, a relationship was formed. Because he answered the call, Israel was led by a mighty prophet of God. In later years, Samuel would be the one to pour the anointing oil on Saul. Further down the line, he would be the one to pour the anointing oil on a young shepherd, named David. It started at this moment when a young man chose to answer the call of the Lord and begin a relationship with Him.

Expect Greater

God Calls. Will You Answer?

Developing a relationship with God starts with answering the call. The Bible says that He stands at our heart's door and knocks. His expectations for us cannot be met without first opening that door and inviting Him into our lives.

Our present and our future depend on this moment. Aligning our desires to His will can only happen when we say, "Yes."

- *Yes, Lord. I choose you.*
- *Yes, Lord. Not only do I choose you, but I choose you above all others.*
- *Yes, Lord. The door to my heart is open. Please, come in and fill me with your Spirit.*
- *Yes, Lord. I confess that I cannot do it alone. I need you in every area of my life.*

Relationship Leads to Intimacy

Just like my earlier example of John's and my relationship, such is our walk with God. God desires intimacy. When referring to our relationship with the Lord, Scripture often uses the metaphor of a bride and her groom. This demonstrates that the intimacy God desires with us comes from a covenant between Him and us.

"Behold, the days come, saith the Lord, that I will make a new covenant with the house of Israel, and with the house of Judah: Not

> *according to the covenant that I made with their fathers in the day that I took them by the hand to bring them out of the land of Egypt; which my covenant they brake, although I was an husband unto them, saith the Lord: But this shall be the covenant that I will make with the house of Israel; After those days, saith the Lord, I will put my law in their inward parts, and write it in their hearts; and will be their God, and they shall be my people. And they shall teach no more every man his neighbour, and every man his brother, saying, Know the Lord: for they shall all know me, from the least of them unto the greatest of them, saith the Lord: for I will forgive their iniquity, and I will remember their sin no more."*
> Jeremiah 31:31-34

From these verses in Jeremiah, we see that God desires a covenant with His people. In the Old Testament, that covenant was with the children of Israel. Now there is a new covenant, as explained in the New Testament, and that relationship is through Jesus Christ.

> *"...at that time [before the cross] ye were without Christ, being aliens from the commonwealth of Israel, and strangers from the covenants of promise, having no hope, and without God in the world: But now in Christ Jesus ye who sometimes were far off are made nigh by the blood of Christ."*

Expect Greater

Ephesians 2:12-13

So, what does this all mean?

God wants a covenant with us regardless of our backgrounds, and this is more than just a marriage contract. As used in Scripture, it's an unbreakable vow that is spiritual. Our covenant with our Creator should not be taken lightly. Deuteronomy 4:24 says that "God is a consuming fire, even a jealous God." Our distractions, our busy lives, and our demands keep us away from pursuing Him pull us away from that deep intimacy God expects.

Developing deep intimacy with God has foundational principles, much like developing deep intimacy with our spouses:

- Deep intimacy cannot be built when there is no trust.
- Deep intimacy needs open communication as a foundation for that trust.
- Deep intimacy needs faithfulness to thrive.
- Deep intimacy involves cherishing each other and reconnecting, especially as the years continue and the newness fades.

Think of attributes that make a marriage more stable and content. Would a spouse appreciate being cheated on? Would a spouse appreciate going days on end without communication and connection? Would a spouse appreciate their significant other so distracted and busy that there is no time for each other? In all actuality, when these negative situations happen in a marriage, hostility, conflict, and relational shutdown can be the result.

Our covenant—or spiritual marriage contract—with God is no different. Being distracted and busy means less time together. Going days and weeks without communication can weaken the relationship (not on God's part, but on ours). A lack of intimacy also means a lack of connectedness. This makes it easier to have a wandering eye and stray.

Through this relationship we receive power that not only blesses us, but also others around us. When in an intimate relationship with God, we learn to discern His voice from others, and we are more open to correction and direction.

> *I exhort therefore, that, first of all, supplications, prayers, intercessions, and giving of thanks, be made for all men; For kings, and for all that are in authority; that we may lead a quiet and peaceable life in all godliness and honesty. For this is good and acceptable in the sight of God our Saviour; Who will have all men to be saved, and to come unto the knowledge of the truth.*
> *1 Timothy 2:1-4*

God's Expectation #4: To Further the Work of His Kingdom

I didn't want to go. There, I said it.

It was 1993, and the Christian college I was attending decided to do a mission trip along the streets of Philadelphia, Pennsylvania. We were going to take sandwiches and the message of salvation. We piled into the buses and drove a couple of hours until we reached our destination.

I remember acting like I was on board with the whole idea, but really, what could I say? The college required regular mission work, and this was one such time. At that point in my life, I was 18, and I did not understand this whole take-the-message-to-the-streets tactic. The way I saw it was that there were churches on practically every street corner. If you wanted Jesus, you had options to choose from.

Don't get me wrong. I was all for ministry inside the church walls. If someone got themselves to church, I was there willing to help in any capacity. I'd volunteered in church nurseries and daycares, I gave Bible studies and taught Sunday School, and I picked people up who needed rides. But going outside the walls? Singing on the streets? Really?

Thanks. I'll pass.

When we arrived, we set up the sandwich and drink stations. We had lunches in bags for those who wanted to take them to go. And the hungry came. It was early in the morning, and I saw homeless coming from benches, some pushing carts or carrying their lives with them in garbage bags. But it was a family of four who broke my heart and changed my mindset.

I didn't start preaching at them nor did I start thumping my Bible, but I remember trying to engage them in conversation. I talked to the children while the parents got bags of food. When they thanked us and began walking away, I wondered what would happen to them. So, I prayed. Right there. It was a quiet, simple prayer, but one that I know was just as powerful as one shouted from a microphone. I simply prayed for that family. I prayed for the children, and that God would take care of them.

Approximately 27 years later, that family still fills my memory as a pointed reminder that God's kingdom is so much more than what happens within the four walls of a church building.

His Kingdom

God sees and knows the B-I-G picture. He gets it. We don't. When we bring our expectations, our desires, and our hopes to Him, much of the time it revolves around us. This is not to say that God does not care about our specific hopes and dreams. Of course, He does! However, He sees our hopes and dreams through His infinite scope and vision. His ultimate purpose is to further His kingdom until it is preached and heard in every land and to every person. Jesus specifically stated that this was His purpose.

> *"...I must preach the kingdom of God to other cities also; for therefore am I sent."*
> *Luke 4:43*

Jesus explained to the Pharisees that "the kingdom of God is in the midst of you," referring to Himself (Luke 17:21), and He spent much of His ministry explaining the kingdom of God through parables. Through these parables, we see and have a better understanding of what the kingdom of God is and what its purpose is.

According to Scripture, the kingdom of God is:
- "...righteousness, and peace, and joy in the Holy Ghost," (Romans 14:17).
- His kingdom has dominion: "The Lord hath prepared his throne in the heavens; and his kingdom ruleth over all," (Psalm 103:19).
- His kingdom is present: "Repent: for the kingdom of heaven is at hand," (Matthew 4:17).
- His kingdom will always be: "Thy kingdom come..." (Matthew 6:10).

When it comes to furthering the kingdom of God, it comes down to other people. What did Jesus say about the two greatest commandments? We are to love God and to love our neighbors. Everything else rests within them.

> *Thou shalt love the Lord thy God with all*

> *thy heart, and with all thy soul, and with all thy mind. This is the first and great commandment. And the second is like unto it, Thou shalt love thy neighbor as thyself. On these commandments hang all the law and the prophets.*
> *Matthew 22: 37-40*

Consider Jesus and His ministry. He didn't choose to enrobe Himself in flesh, take on the suffering of the world, and die a horrific, bloody death for his own self-serving benefit. "For even the Son of man came not to be ministered unto, but to minister, and to give his life a ransom for many," (Mark 10:45).

Everything He did was for us. Everything. His sacrifice was required for His kingdom to include us. Being like Christ means that we are His ambassadors doing His will on earth. Paul explains this in II Corinthians 5:20, where he says, "Now then we are ambassadors for Christ, as though God did beseech you by us: we pray you in Christ's stead, be ye reconciled to God."

- *Okay*, you may say, *so where does our will fit in?*

Or, other variations:

- *What are you trying to say, Janice? That I can't desire anything for my own life that doesn't include helping other people?*
- *Doesn't God give us the desires of our heart? What if our desires have nothing to do with other people?*
- *What's wrong with wanting a better, easier life?*
- *What about if I have a specific need? Does God not care about that?*

All of these questions have merit and are worthy of an answer. Here it is: God does care about us, and each of our needs are important to Him. Nothing is too big or too small for God to handle. When we have a relationship with Him, our lives begin to align with His will and purpose. At some point, certain things won't matter as much to you as they used to. He will begin to work with you on your perspective. Your eyes will hopefully be opened to every blessing in your life, and how to turn and give freely to others in a way that glorifies God. That means being kingdom-minded.

Being Kingdom-Minded

God's expectation to further His kingdom means that we must be kingdom-minded. Paul states in I Corinthians 10:31, "Whether therefore ye eat, or drink, or whatsoever ye do, do all to the glory of God." If your dream or vision involves placing yourself on a pedestal or something where you feel more significant or validated, search your motives. James 4:3 warns that "Ye ask, and receive not, because ye ask amiss, that ye may consume it upon your lusts." The Contemporary English translation of this Scripture says, "You ask and don't receive because you ask with wrong motives, so that you may spend it on your pleasures." Basically, God sees and judges our hearts. And simply stated, our dreams may not be aligned with God's plans for our lives.

Think of Jesus praying in the Garden of Gethsemane. He knew what was about to happen. He already understood His purpose on earth. Yet He still prayed and asked it not to happen.

Expect Greater

And [Jesus] went a little further, and fell on his face, and prayed, saying, O my Father, if it be possible, let this cup pass from me: nevertheless not as I will, but as thou wilt.
Matthew 26:39

Jesus' powerful example shows exactly what it means to be kingdom-minded. He prayed, He requested, then He simply stated, "nevertheless not as I will, but as thou wilt." Some of us need to have that "nevertheless" moment in our prayer time with the Lord. When we say "nevertheless not my will, but yours…" we are truly becoming more kingdom-minded.

There are four specific take-aways when endeavoring to be kingdom-minded: being selfless, having the heart of a servant, denying our flesh, and going against our will.

Being Kingdom-Minded means being empathetic.

I've always enjoyed baking, and my family enjoys the finished products. When my youngest son, Benjamin, was around four, he kept sneaking warm cookies from the cooling rack. I noticed him sneak one or two, and at first, I thought it was cute. "No more," I told him. "These are for the church banquet." As I got busy again, I didn't think any more about it. That is until another batch came out of the oven. I went to place the cookies on the cooling rack and noticed several cookies missing. I also noticed Ben sitting under the table with his mouth full!

"Benjamin!" I scolded. "I told you no more cookies."

"Why?" he asked. "I like them."

"I know you like them, but these aren't for you."

"But I want them."

I decided to try a different tactic. "If you eat all the cookies, there won't be any left for the church party."

Benjamin shrugged and simply said, "I'm okay with that."

My son had no problem inconveniencing other people because in his four-year-old brain he wanted the cookies and that was what mattered. We know, as parents, that it is our responsibility to teach our children about empathy and what it means to think about other people. However, if we truly were being honest, we might admit how easy it is to think and behave selfishly.

God's will is not based on our selfish motives, but instead, His will is to further His kingdom. Most of the time, our dreams and future aspirations tend to be self-centered. Self-preservation is not necessarily a bad thing or a sinful thing. Wanting the best in our lives and the lives of our families makes us human. God wants the best for us too.

So, why is there a disparity?

There doesn't have to be. Protecting and providing for ourselves and our families does not have to get in the way of empathy. Empathy is simply a consideration for other people and their feelings. Being kingdom-minded means that lifting up others and giving of our time and talents is an integral part of our walk with the Lord. When He is first in our lives, others will definitely notice. In John 3:30, John the Baptist states what needs to be said and applied even today: "He [meaning Jesus] must increase; I must decrease."

We might be looking at all of the "cookies" that we want

in our lives and find ourselves questioning God. "Why can't we have all the cookies?" However, furthering the kingdom of God on earth means that just because we want something doesn't make it ours. It also does not mean that God is obligated to grant our request. Truly being kingdom-minded means that we will be content with the blessings in our own lives and practice empathy by endeavoring to be a blessing in other people's lives.

Being kingdom-minded means having the heart of a servant.

Servants serve. Seems simple, right? Our lives, as followers of Christ, are to minister. Ministry is service. It's more than the pulpit. More than titles. More than distinguished honors. Our denominations have, at times, strayed far from the purpose of ministry. We've begun to idolize the pulpit and those who stand behind it. People will travel long distances to hear certain preachers as if God only talks to them. We place these men and women on pedestals that they are not meant to be on, and then if we're not careful, we covet their prestige and the power that comes with it.

When God calls us, it is not a calling toward comfort. It's a calling that separates us from the world. It's a calling that draws us out from our past and sets us on a path of purpose. That path of purpose starts with service. If our expectations for our lives revolve around us, then we are not yet kingdom-minded. In Luke chapter 9, Jesus told the disciples to go and "proclaim the kingdom of God and to heal the sick." Yet He wasn't done with His instructions. He told them: "Take nothing for the journey—no staff, no bag, no bread, no money, no extra shirt." Jesus expected them to stay with others until it was time to leave that town. These disciples, by setting aside their comfort, did exactly what Jesus commanded of them. The result? The news of Jesus spread.

When the disciples came back from their travels, Jesus ministered to large crowds and continued to perform miracles. Would that have happened if the disciples hadn't been obedient? Once alone with His disciples, Jesus clarifies His kingdom:

---

*"...If any man will come after me, **let him deny himself**, and take up his cross daily, and follow me. For whosoever will save his life shall lose it: but whosoever will lose his life for my sake, the same shall save it. For what is a man advantaged, if he gain the whole world, and lose himself, or be cast away?"*
Luke 9:23-25

I do question this era we live in, and how Jesus fits into our busy, first-world lives. Even our churches have turned into mega-businesses with traveling preachers and so-called "pastors" who have been elevated to such high positions that they are almost celebrities in their church circles. Let us pray that God in His compassion continues to remind us that His expectations are not so much for us to be elevated to positions of power and prestige, but to daily humble ourselves before Him and remember that service is the requirement.

Being kingdom-minded often means denying our flesh.

Our flesh is sinful. We were born into sin, and none of us are naturally righteous. On the contrary, our righteousness is "as filthy rags." In Romans 8:7, Paul says "The carnal mind is enmity against God; for it is not subject to the law of God, neither indeed can be." This means that our flesh, or "carnal mind," is hostile toward God and refuses to surrender to the laws of God because it is unable to do so. No matter how hard we try, we will never measure up to the holiness and righteousness of Jesus Christ.

Do you see why Jesus tells us that if we are to follow Him, we must die to our flesh daily and take up our crosses? Dying to our flesh is no easy feat. Just as Jesus died, our flesh must die in the spiritual sense. The new birth experience, as Jesus discussed with Nicodemus in John chapter 3, is critical, and it is the place to start. Once we've repented and surrendered our lives over to the Lord through baptism in His name and receiving His spirit, a powerful, supernatural event takes place, transforming our inner man. As most of us know, this is not the end of our battle with the flesh. We can be born again and completely surrendered, yet still be tempted. That is why denying our flesh is a daily mindset, and one that requires a committed, consistent relationship with Jesus Christ.

Denying our flesh puts God first, which sets the stage for truly great things to happen, not just in our own lives, but in the lives of others around us. When God is truly front and center, our selfish gains mean a lot less, and blessing others by being a servant brings peace and ultimate joy. This, my friends, is truly being kingdom-minded.

Being kingdom-minded often goes against our wills.

King Saul's son, Jonathan, was willing to step aside from the throne, even though he was the heir apparent. He trusted God's plan over his own desires. Furthering the work of God's kingdom often means setting aside what we want and becoming aligned with what God wants. It is never about us, but it is all about Him reaching others. This is an important point because when we truly tap into the heartbeat of God and allow ourselves to be His vessel, we can change the lives of so many people.

Furthering God's Kingdom doesn't mean we're a Doormat

A note about boundaries: Being kingdom-minded does not mean that we must allow others to walk all over us. Boundaries are a necessity for God's kingdom to be fulfilled through us. How so? Even Jesus left his disciples often to go and be alone. He needed time to be by Himself to recharge. He also had no problem telling people exactly what He thought. He didn't mince words or worry about offending someone by stating the truth.

If we're not careful, we can become so focused on kingdom-work that we become frazzled or burned out. Please remember that God knows our limitations and does not want our own well-being to suffer. Saying "no" doesn't necessarily mean that you are selfish or focused on your own needs. The key is to be in a prayerful relationship with Christ. He will lead you and direct you.

Final Thoughts

God's expectations push us to think outside of ourselves. His will is that none should perish, which means that we have work to do. When we are in alignment with Him, then His will becomes ours. When His will becomes ours, that is truly being kingdom-minded.

> *For I know the thoughts that I think toward you,*
> *saith the Lord, thoughts of peace, and not of evil,*
> *to give you <u>an expected end.</u>*
> *Then shall ye call upon me,*
> *and ye shall go and pray unto me,*
> *and I will hearken unto you.*
> *And ye shall seek me, and find me, when ye shall search for me with all your heart.*
> *Jeremiah 29:11-13*

God's Expectation #5: To Trust His Provision

Let's be real. Sometimes God doesn't make a lot of sense to us.

It didn't make sense to me or my husband that God would keep us somewhere for years, even though we were both miserable. It didn't make sense that God would answer our prayers for a second child, only to find out at 18 weeks gestation that the baby had died in the womb. It didn't make sense for God to take my mother from my life before I could ever say good-bye.

Each of us probably has personal accounts of situations in our lives that simply do not make sense in the grand scheme of things. This past year, I intentionally prayed for financial freedom. There were several areas I struggled with, and I was determined, with God's help, to overcome and conquer the debt. As soon as I began to fast, everything seemed to go wrong at the same time. I had two book contracts pulled, my place of employment informed me that they had overpaid me and needed approximately $4,000 immediately, and then the engine blew on my Chevy Traverse, a car that I only owned for 2.5 years and still paid the car note. The engine replacement would cost about $8,000. Talk about frustrated!

I struggled with Jeremiah 29:11, the part where God

explains His plans to bless and help us. At that moment, I felt discouraged and alone. I did not feel prosperous. In all honesty, I felt defeated and overwhelmed.

As long as I stayed focused on my distress and troubles, I fell more and more into despair. Through tears, I begged God that if He wasn't going to change my circumstances to at least change my perspective. "Help me see things as you see them."

That simple prayer opened my eyes to His provision. I had to prepare for a Sunday School lesson that same week, and the lesson was on 1 Kings 17:

> *And it came to pass after a while, that the brook dried up, because there had been no rain in the land. And the word of the LORD came unto him, saying, Arise, get thee to Zarephath, which belongeth to Zidon, and dwell there: behold, I have commanded a widow woman there to sustain thee. So he arose and went to Zarephath. And when he came to the gate of the city, behold, the widow woman was there gathering of sticks: and he called to her, and said, Fetch me, I pray thee, a little water in a vessel, that I may drink. And as she was going to fetch it, he called to her, and said, Bring me, I pray thee, a morsel of bread in thine hand. And she said, As the LORD thy God liveth, I have not a cake, but an handful of meal in a barrel, and a little oil in a cruse: and, behold, I am gathering two sticks, that I may go in and dress it for me and my son, that we may eat it, and die.*

This widow's circumstances were horrific. She had enough flour and oil for one more meal. Their outlook was dire. Death was imminent. Doing what the Lord asked did not make sense. At that present moment, it was making her already dire situation worse, yet her decision to trust God and obey His instruction led to provision. The drought lasted for years, but every day the widow found enough flour and oil to live.

> *And Elijah said to her, Fear not; go and do as thou hast said: but make me thereof a little cake first, and bring it unto me, and after make for thee and for thy son. For thus saith the LORD God of Israel, The barrel of meal shall not waste, neither shall the cruse of oil fail, until the day that the LORD sendeth rain upon the earth. And she went and did according to the saying of Elijah: and she, and he, and her house, did eat many days. And the barrel of meal wasted not, neither did the cruse of oil fail, according to the word of the LORD, which he spake by Elijah.*
> *1 Kings 17*

As I prepared the Sunday School lesson, I felt immediate conviction. Not only did I begin to thank God for His provision in my life, but I also knew, just as the widow of Zarephath, I had a decision to make. Would I trust and obey God when my situation overwhelmed me? Would I choose to see His hand of provision in my life regardless of the circumstances?

The Meaning of Jeremiah 29:11

Prosperity, in and of itself, means different things. Some of us may connect it to prospering in our finances or our possessions, but what are possessions when you are sick? What amount of money will truly keep you safe in times of adversity? Steve Jobs, the co-founder of Apple, was a billionaire, yet died too soon at the age of 56. His money mattered little as cancer spread through him. We all probably know of families or individuals struggling in some capacity. I have dear friends whose daughter is medically-fragile, and their lives completely revolve around her care. My friend told me that she feels overwhelmed and shut-in. On the other hand, she loves her daughter fiercely and knows that until the Lord intervenes, this is her "normal."

I mention these examples because we can be very spoiled and ungrateful for true prosperity in our lives. It isn't until something happens and we are faced with a deficit in some area (health, resources, etc.), that we may truly begin to appreciate everything that God's "prosperity" encompasses. Consider these areas:

- Food
- Shelter
- Another day to live
- A family
- Friends
- God's creation
- Our salvation through Him
- The hope of heaven
- Peace of mind
- Joy of heart

So, now, answer me this: what is prosperity? In what ways do you already "prosper?" Is that not the Lord's provision?

When I lived in Northern Michigan, I endured much stress. It was a difficult time, and I often felt very isolated. On top of that, I had a health condition that was worsening (because of the stress), and my son, Jonathan, was showing signs of some sort of language disability. My heart was in a continual state of heaviness. I prayed, and prayed, and prayed. I cried. I begged God. I would quote Jeremiah 29:11 like an anthem flying over my life, but I continued to struggle. Actually, things got worse.

And I didn't get it.

I didn't get how God could make all these promises and not deliver. I didn't understand how He could simply ignore my prayers. I even asked Him in my desperation: "Are you even real? If so, where are you?"

Did God send me some great revelation? Nope.

Did the clouds part, as His voice rang from the heavens to my soul? Nope.

Instead, I struggled with second child infertility. And then, when I became pregnant after years of trying, I lost the baby at 18 weeks gestation. I delivered my baby boy in a small room in the ER, feeling more alone and broken than ever before.

Where was this prosperity that Jeremiah 29:11 promised?

Now, as I look back on those times, I see things much more clearly, but going through it often blurs spiritual vision. So, let me lay it out for you: during that overwhelming, discouraging time in my life, God's blessings were all around me. I simply failed to see them. I was so consumed with my situation and everyday battles that I forgot to look up.

I'm not saying that I didn't deserve to be upset and to grieve over the circumstances, but when we have the right perspective, we don't dwell in that moment. We see the goodness of the Lord and trust that He is working it out for the good. It's easier to say than to actually put into practice. After I lost my child, I struggled with depression and grief for a long time. Yet when we weren't expecting it, my husband and I learned that I was pregnant again. Fourteen months after losing our child, I delivered a healthy baby boy. Benjamin David came into our world a miracle, and he is a daily reminder of the promise of Jeremiah 29:11.

Let's not wait until a storm comes our way to see the blessings we've been given! Let's see God's blessings now. That way, His true gifts of prosperity won't be lost on us.

Final Thoughts

God's will doesn't always make sense, but His plan is to prosper us and to use our prosperity to bless others. The key is to understand what prosperity means and what it does not mean. Life may be difficult, but when we are walking in the will of the Lord, prosperity and protection are part of the equation.

> *And if I go and prepare a place for you, I will come again, and receive you unto myself; that where I am, there ye may be also.*
> *John 14:3*

God's Expectations #6: To Get Us Ready for Eternity

My parents drove a station wagon for most of my childhood. There were four of us kids, and we'd pile in. A couple of us always chose to climb over the seat and sit in the back. On one such evening on our way to Sunday evening service, my brother and I were in the back of the station wagon. I was young enough to fall asleep in the back, as was my brother.

I woke up to darkness and a thunderstorm.

Paul woke up beside me, and we both began to freak out.

Why?

Simple. The rapture must have taken place, and we had been left behind.

A little farfetched, but as church kids, we'd been warned about the perils of hell, as well as the importance of making sure we were ready to go when that trumpet sounded. How had I missed the trumpet? It bothered me that my parents and my sisters had vanished. (And I couldn't figure out how my sisters made it, and I got left behind. There's no way they could have gotten into heaven with some of their antics.)

Expect Greater

Eventually, Paul and I noticed the lights on through the sanctuary windows and saw the people inside.

We know the Bible says to be ready. We know it says that Jesus is returning for His bride. We know it, but do we believe it?

This life is but a vapor. Still, it consumes us.

As I write this, the coronavirus has taken over our nation. Everything is shut down. We are all ordered to stay at home. It's uncertain times. Fear and panic are palpable. Citizens are overstocking to the point that there is nothing left for others.

It's sounding the alarm in my soul.

We are so worried about death, yet we completely ignore the eternal. Even those of us who don't ignore the eternal still struggle with being too focused on the *here and now*.

The fact remains that none of us will live forever in these mortal bodies. From the moment we are born, we march toward physical death. Forgive me for sounding morbid, but we need to be reminded of this truth because then it helps us understand what Paul meant when he wrote, "God has not given us the spirit of fear…" God is not afraid of sickness or death. He is not worried about tomorrow. He knows that this life on earth passes only too quickly. It is eternity that is forever.

Eternity is our home.

God's expectations are for His people to ready themselves and to ready others for eternity. His will is that no one perishes. Jesus said, "…I go to prepare a place for you…That where I am there you may be also," (John 14:2-3).

We must align our dreams and goals to His ultimate purpose: to be a light and draw others to Him. Selfishly pursuing our dreams and desires can have dire effects on our relationship with Him and whether or not He will say to us, "Well done, thou good and faithful servant."

The Rich Man and Lazarus

Jesus spent a lot of time warning us about the need to align our will and desires with the eternal.

> *There was a certain rich man, which was clothed in purple and fine linen, and fared sumptuously every day: And there was a certain beggar named Lazarus, which was laid at his gate, full of sores, And desiring to be fed with the crumbs which fell from the rich man's table: moreover the dogs came and licked his sores.*
> *And it came to pass, that the beggar died, and was carried by the angels into Abraham's bosom: the rich man also died, and was buried; And in hell he lift up his eyes, being in torments, and seeth Abraham afar off, and Lazarus in his bosom. And he cried and said, Father Abraham, have mercy on me, and send Lazarus, that he may dip the tip of his finger in water, and cool my tongue; for I am tormented in this flame. But Abraham said, Son, remember that thou in thy lifetime receivedst thy good things, and likewise Lazarus evil things: but now he is comforted, and thou art tormented. And beside all this, between us and you there is a great gulf fixed: so that they which would pass from hence to you cannot; neither can they pass to us, that would come from*

thence.
Luke 16:19-26

In this example, Jesus explains the parable about the rich man and a poor beggar named Lazarus. From this parable, it is clear that there are two very different places, and that once we die in the physical, we are still alive in the eternal. More so, this parable is a warning that where we end up is determined by our actions and decisions on earth.

Eternity with Jesus

God's will for us is to spend eternity with Him. That's the end goal. Not only for us to spend eternity with Him, but for us to lead others to spend eternity with Him. John 3:16 can't get any clearer: "For God so loved the world that He gave His only begotten son, that whosoever believeth in Him should not perish but have everlasting life." So, His expectations are for us to believe in Him, and in so doing, to have everlasting life.

What do we know about belief? What does it mean to "believe in Him?"

- "He that believeth on me, as the scripture hath said, out of his belly shall flow rivers of living water," (John 7:38).
- "He that believeth and is baptized shall be saved; but he that believeth not shall be damned," (Mark 16:16).
- "Verily, verily, I say unto thee, Except a man be born of water and of the Spirit, he cannot enter into the kingdom of God," (John 3:5).
- "...Verily, verily, I say unto you, He that believeth on

me, the works that I do shall he do also; and greater works than these shall he do; because I go unto my Father," (John 14:12).
- "If ye love me, keep my commandments," (John 14:15).
- "…Faith without works is dead," (James 2:20).

All of these examples are like puzzle pieces that show us a clear picture of God's expectations for our lives. His expectations for us involve not only believing in Him but also displaying the evidence of that belief.

Our Salvation Story

Think of your salvation story. Who led you to the faith? I was blessed to be raised in the faith, so my salvation story starts with my mom. She worked at Kroger in the early 1970s, and there was a woman there talking about a church she'd been attending. This woman decided to be baptized and asked my mom to go to the service with her. My mom went and ended up getting baptized too! She went home and told my dad who decided to go with her to the next service, and he was also baptized. He told me that he came up out of the water speaking in tongues, and his life forever changed.

I wish I knew who the lady was who asked my mom to go to church. I want to hug her neck and thank her. Our family was forever changed because that woman made a decision about her eternity and shared the good news with my mom, thus starting a chain reaction.

Some may not have heard the gospel, or at least not in its entirety. Think about children who grow up in homes where

Expect Greater

God is never discussed. They grow up to see churches on corners or may run into people who are "believers," but they have not been in an environment that shares the full gospel with them.

For others, it's a situation like the rich young ruler of Matthew. They desire Jesus, but not enough to let go of their past and their worldly desires.

Then some are skeptical. The good news has been shared with them, but they don't believe it.

In Matthew 13, Jesus provides a parable that better explains this kingdom principle:

> *And he spake many things unto them in parables, saying, Behold, a sower went forth to sow; And when he sowed, some seeds fell by the way side, and the fowls came and devoured them up: Some fell upon stony places, where they had not much earth: and forthwith they sprung up, because they had no deepness of earth: And when the sun was up, they were scorched; and because they had no root, they withered away. And some fell among thorns; and the thorns sprung up, and choked them: But other fell into good ground, and brought forth fruit, some an hundredfold, some sixtyfold, some thirtyfold. Who hath ears to hear, let him hear.*
> *Matthew 13:3-9*

When the word goes forth, it's up to us what we do with it. I've been asked variations of this question throughout my adult life: If God is so good, and if He loves us so much, why does He send us to hell?

Newsflash: hell was not created for humanity. Hell was created for Satan and his angels. God's desire, as detailed in Scripture, has always been for us to dwell with Him in the eternal. Jesus said, "I go to prepare a place for you."

Final Thoughts

The here and now often takes my focus and energy, and my spiritual life, the side of me that knows and understands that there is a heaven and a hell, is set on the backburner. It's almost as if my mindset is, "I'll worry about that another day."

Unfortunately, not one of us is promised tomorrow, yet we make plans like we're going to live forever. We feel slighted when death comes to those around us, especially when it wasn't expected, or when it happens too soon. Our grief is understandable. In John 11, when Jesus finally visits his friend, Lazarus, who died from sickness, the Bible states that "Jesus wept." Grief is real and palpable, and it only intensifies when we feel death has robbed us of our loved ones.

But death is not the end.

Read that again.

Death. Is. Not. The. End.

We live on, and from what Scripture implies and/or directly states, God's expectation is for us to do what is necessary to make sure we spend eternity with Him. Not only that but He expects that we share the Good News and bring people with us.

Part II: Derailing God's Expectations

> ***And say unto him, Take heed, and be quiet; fear not, neither be fainthearted...***
>
> ***Isaiah 7:4***

Derailment #1: Falling into Fear

I wasn't supposed to watch *Jaws*. But my friend's parents weren't as strict. So, we watched Jaws, and I remember being terrified. To this day, I don't like swimming in the ocean or even in lakes if the water depth is over my head.

It's irrational, and I realize that. But that's fear.

There are times when a healthy dose of fear or apprehension keeps us from doing anything too risky. Heights flip my stomach, and for that reason, you won't see me on the roofs of towering buildings balancing on the ledge. There are varying degrees of fear from butterflies in the stomach to the sleep-robbing, panic-filled kind. If we're not careful, fear can take over our lives and derail our divine purpose.

Two Kinds of Fear

There are two main branches of fear: fear as reverence, and fear as reactionary. These determine the trajectory of our lives. One honors God, and the other is not of God. One serves the Lord, the other serves the flesh. God's purpose for our lives is fulfilled when we fear Him, but it is derailed when we entertain and embrace the spirit of fear. It's imperative we know and understand this difference.

> *For God hath not given us the spirit of fear; but of power, and of love, and of a sound mind.*
> *2 Timothy 1:7*

First and foremost, there is the fear of the Lord, which is required of every believer. This is not fear in terms of *fright* or *terror*, but fear as respect to the one in authority over our lives. Think of it this way: when we were children, we probably had a healthy fear of our parents, even though we probably felt safest with them. We were not *afraid* of our parents, but we understood that they made the rules and expected us to honor the rules. These rules were meant for our protection. The same is true with our Heavenly Father.

The Bible mentions this *reverent* fear several times:

1. "The fear of the Lord is the beginning of wisdom; a good understanding have all they that do His commandments," (Psalm 111:10).
2. "And walking in the fear of the Lord and in the comfort of the Holy Spirit, they were multiplied," (Acts 9:31).
3. "The fear of the Lord is the beginning of knowledge," (Proverbs 1:7).
4. "Come, you children, listen to me; I will teach you the fear of the Lord…Keep your tongue from evil, and your lips from speaking deceit. Depart from evil and do good; seek peace and pursue it," Psalm 34: 11, 13-14.
5. "Do not let your heart envy sinners, but be zealous

for the fear of the LORD all the day; for surely there is a hereafter, and your hope will not be cut off," (Proverbs 23:17-18).
6. "The fear of the LORD is a fountain of life, to turn one away from the snares of death," (Proverbs 14:27).
7. "The fear of the LORD leads to life, and he who has it will abide in satisfaction; he will not be visited with evil," (Proverbs 19:23).

From these verses, it is clear that fearing the Lord brings about Godly wisdom and knowledge, as well as provides hope for our future through a blessed and peaceful life. So, when we revere and honor the Lord, His blessings rain upon us, and those blessings multiply to those around us.

The second type is a spirit of fear, and it's not of God. The spirit of fear is a poor substitute for Godly fear. This cowardly spirit brings about anxiety and depression. It tricks us into losing sleep and simply giving up. The spirit of fear upsets our health: our mental health, physical health, and spiritual health. In I John 4:18, this type of fear "hath torment."

This tormenting fear binds us like chains. Romans 8:15 says as much: "For you did not receive the spirit of bondage again to fear..." And Hebrews 2:15 says that those who fear are subjected to a lifetime of bondage. Another translation of this verse in Hebrews shows that this type of fear holds us in slavery.

In essence, the spirit of fear can be summed up:
1. It's not of God.
2. It torments us.
3. It's cowardly.

4. It keeps us bound (like a slave).

See the difference? The next section speaks specifically of the spirit of fear and how it wreaks havoc in our lives.

Recognizing Fear for What It Is

Fear is dysfunctional. It sabotages God's will for us by creating a climate of worry and doubt and destroying our peace in Christ. When we fall into fear, bad decisions are made, such as decisions of self-preservation. This is blatantly saying that we don't trust God to take care of us and to lead us to the best possible life.

Jesus warned us of this fear in Matthew 25. In verses 14 through 30, Jesus expounds upon the parable of the three servants who each received talents from their master. The first two servants took the talents given to them and grew those talents into more. This pleased the master. The third servant, however, did things a little differently because he was afraid:

> *Then he which had received the one talent came and said, Lord, I knew thee that thou art a hard man...**And I was afraid,** and went and hid thy talent in the earth: lo, there thou has that is thine.*
> *Matthew 25:24-25*

Because the third servant was overcome by fear, he made a poor decision. His decision not only displeased the master, but it brought about judgment and consequences:

> *His lord answered and said unto him, Thou wicked and slothful servant...cast ye the unprofitable servant into outer darkness: there shall be weeping and gnashing of teeth.*
> *Matthew 25:26, 30*

If that sounds pretty harsh, then what about Revelation 21:8? This verse says that the "fearful" will not inherit the kingdom. Why such punishment?

When we give in to fear, we are disobeying God's command to "Fear not." These two words are specifically stated over 70 times in Scripture (per the KJV). And in God's eyes, "...to obey is better than sacrifice..." (I Samuel 15:22). We cannot embrace and entertain the spirit of fear in our lives, while out of the same mouth pronounce that we live for the Lord. We cannot live in disobedience to the Word of God—by giving into fear—yet expect God's purpose in our lives to be fulfilled.

Fear blocks God's expectations for our lives.

When we're fearful, our eyes are off of God and His provision. Just look at the children of Israel and observe God's frustration and anger when they continually fell back into fear and worry. When the twelve spies came back and reported on the promised land, only two—Joshua and Caleb—saw the blessings and promise being fulfilled. The other ten complained and were afraid, and because of that, they did not get to experience God's promise.

The list continues. King Saul. Gideon. Peter. Just to name a few.

Expect Greater

All three faced fear. King Saul continued to let it rule his heart. He lost his mind and instead of living peaceably with David, he chased him like a dog and ended up dying a horrible death at the hands of Israel's mortal enemy.

Gideon and Peter did not let fear derail them for long. In Judges 6 and 7, Gideon struggled to understand why God would choose him to lead Israel in the victory against the Midianites. If Gideon had continued to live in fear, he would have refused God's calling. The miracle that took place where 300 Israelites defeated over 100,000 enemy soldiers may not have happened. However, Gideon shook off the fear and trusted the Lord. That great victory is remembered and talked about thousands of years later.

Look at Peter. For three years, he walked alongside the Messiah. He witnessed miracle after miracle. He experienced walking on water and Lazarus rising from the dead. And then everything changed. Jesus was taken into custody, beaten, tortured, and sentenced to a humiliating death on the cross. Fear led Peter to cutting off a soldier's ear and to denying Jesus three times to protect himself. Yet Peter sought forgiveness, and God used him to usher in a mighty revival, as seen in the book of Acts.

What do these examples show us?

Simply this: Fear causes hasty decisions and blocks Gods' direction.

Final Thoughts

There's a reason why the Bible is filled with God reminding His people not to be afraid. It is easy to fall into fear. Life is unpredictable. We make plans, only for those plans to be paused. Sudden sickness or crisis can rock our worlds, and in an instant, the spirit of fear is present, ready to derail God's plans for us. Fear also manifests itself in other ways. Worry, doubt, and anxiety are all branches of the same vine, and that vine is fear. Recognize fear—and all its manifestations—for what it is and rebuke it from your life. Don't let it rob your peace, and refuse to give in to it when pursuing God-given dreams. We must daily reset our minds to not look at present circumstances but to set our sights on the one who has us in the palm of His hand.

Derailment #2: Seeking & Justifying Our Own Lusts

Many of us are good at justifying our decisions and actions in life.

Do you want to leave your marriage? The world tells you to do it.

Do you want to pursue intimacy with and cohabitate with someone to whom you're not married? Sure, go for it. The world tells you that you should 'try out' a partner before a lifelong commitment.

Do you want to get ahead at your job? Then use people and tear them down around others. Build yourself up, no matter who you trample on.

For those who are unbelievers, this horrible advice might make sense. We are bombarded with images and messages that promote the justification of selfishness and pleasure. The motto, *if it feels good, do it*, is popular for that reason. That's enough justification for a lot of people.

What's the result? Brokenness and unrealized potential. Misery and depression. Suicidal thoughts and alienation. Children growing up in broken homes, and then repeating the cycle because it's all they know. Sexual diseases running rampant. The beauty of marital union ripped apart and viewed as repressive. Unapologetic sinful lifestyles. And on and on the list goes…

This self-centeredness, however, should have no place among the saints of God, yet it does.

Biblical Examples

Abraham and Sarah were given the promise of an heir, but as the years passed, Sarah decided that Abraham should marry Hagar, her maidservant. There is no Biblical record of her asking God about this idea, only her justifying the decision to her husband. Sarah should have birthed Abraham's firstborn, but instead, Hagar birthed Ishmael. Sarah was immediately jealous of Hagar and her son. What resulted was tremendous turmoil and conflict that is still felt to this day.

Ananias and Sapphira, in the book of Acts, justified their decision to keep some of the money from the sale of their property. They didn't seek God's direction. They justified between themselves that they were still giving to the saints, so what's a little bit for themselves? God killed both of them for their deception.

Esau justified that his immediate hunger was more important than his birthright. He ended up being robbed and stripped of it all.

David justified sleeping with Uriah's wife because his friend was not around to stop him. This decision led to David covering up his sin by killing his friend. The child produced from that sin died, and the sword never left David's house. Not only did the baby die, but three of David's sons died horrific deaths, and David was powerless to stop it.

Eve justified eating the fruit. In Genesis 3:12, Adam justified his actions by blaming someone else: "The woman whom thou gavest to be with me, she gave me of the tree, and I did eat." In the next verse, Eve justified her actions by blaming someone else: "The serpent beguiled me, and I did eat." Adam was punished for his actions, as was Eve, as was the serpent.

God ordered King Saul to utterly destroy the Amalekites, yet Saul chooses to keep Agag (the Amalekite king) alive, as well as collect all the spoils from the war. This was a clear violation of God's instructions, yet when Samuel approached Saul about God's displeasure, Saul justified disobeying God in three distinct ways. First, he justifies his actions by saying that his decision was to honor God: "They have brought them from the Amalekites: for the people spared the best of the sheep and of the oxen, to sacrifice unto the Lord thy God; and the rest we have utterly destroyed," (I Samuel 15:15). When Samuel wasn't buying the excuse, Saul moved to his second excuse, which was to say that he didn't do it, others did: "the people took of the spoil, sheep and oxen, the chief of the things which should have been utterly destroyed..." (verse 21). When King Saul heard that God no longer wanted him to be king, Saul still tried to justify his actions by blaming peer pressure: "I have sinned: for I have transgressed the commandment of the Lord, and thy words: because I feared the people, and obeyed their voice," (verse 24).

All of these examples endured dire consequences that negatively affected the rest of their lives.

After all the miracles that the Children of Israel saw with their own eyes (parting of the Red Sea, water from a rock, manna from heaven), they still struggled with simply obeying God's instruction. There was a clear path to the Promised Land, but the Children of Israel wandered the desert for forty years because of their disobedience, disgruntled attitudes, and disregard for the Godly leadership in their lives. The selfish decisions of the Children of Israel cost them time and lives. First, they justified their complaints. They justified their idol worship, their contempt for their leadership, and they justified their desire for more. Every time the children of Israel came up with excuses and complaints, they justified among themselves that they had a right to feel that way.

Moral of the Story

The quickest way to fall out of alignment with God's will is to simply do things your way. Staying under the authority of God protects us. When we don't seek God first, or when we don't align ourselves with the Word of God, it is a surefire way to bring about life situations that we were never supposed to endure.

One night of pleasure may lead to disease or raising a child alone.

One affair may ruin a life built between a husband and wife and destroy the family unit.

One angry outburst may lead to others looking at you differently or a closed-door to that promotion you wanted.

One moment of deception may cost you a job or friends.

In Judges 21:25, the Bible describes what happens when there is no king or master ruling over us: "…every man did that which was right in his own eyes." The result was chaos and sin then, and it is chaos and sin today.

Crucify the Flesh

The lust of the flesh, the lust of the eye, and the pride of life are a temptation for all of us. Just because we are Christians does not make us immune to these sins. When we pursue selfish goals and put ourselves first, we are choosing to operate in the flesh. Not only must we overcome these temptations, but seeking our own lusts and desires takes us outside the will of God, bringing a screeching halt to God's plans for us.

Our flesh is enmity against God. Selfish gain, hedonism, covetousness, self-centeredness and apathy, hostility and hatred, all of this is a stench in the nostrils of our Savior. Seeking our own lusts goes directly against God's plan. We have to recognize it so that we can stop it before it starts. The Bible is very clear about God's displeasure with our fleshly lusts, as well as His expectation for us to resist these desires of the flesh:

- "For all that is in the world, the lust of the flesh, the lust of the eyes, and the pride of life, is not of the Father but is of the world." 1 John 2:16 "And the world passeth away, and the lust thereof: but he that doeth the will of God abideth forever." Verse 17.
- "Dearly beloved, I beseech you as strangers and pilgrims, abstain from fleshly lusts, which war against the soul." 1 Peter 2:11
- "Instead, clothe yourselves with the Lord Jesus Christ, and make no provision for the desires of the flesh." Romans 13:14

- "Among whom also we all had our conversation in times past in the lusts of our flesh, fulfilling the desires of the flesh and of the mind." Ephesians 2:3
- "This I say then, Walk in the Spirit, and ye shall not fulfill the lust of the flesh." Galatians 5:16
- "Now the works of the flesh are manifest, which are these; Adultery, fornication, uncleanness, lasciviousness Idolatry, witchcraft, hatred, variance, emulations, wrath, strife, seditions, heresies, Envyings, murders, drunkenness, revellings, and such like: of the which I tell you before, as I have also told you in time past, that they which do such things shall not inherit the kingdom of God". Galatians 5:19-21
- "Therefore to him that knoweth to do good, and doeth it not, to him it is sin." James 4:17

Since the Bible is blatantly clear about resisting the flesh and dying to it daily, why do we justify ourselves and our flesh when it fits our agenda?

- Why do we abhor abortion, yet turn our nose up when it comes to serving those living in poverty? When have we served *the least of these*?
- Why do we rail against prejudice, yet gossip about those within our church community?
- Why do we judge others' sinful lifestyles, yet fail to remove *the beam out of our own eye*?
- Why do we make poor decisions, yet blame others for those decisions?

All of these questions raise awareness of how easily we justify our thoughts and actions, even when they go against Scripture. This mirrors the Pharisees behavior in the Gospels. Jesus called them out on their wrongful justification time and time again. When they were getting ready to stone an adulteress woman, Jesus stopped them: "He that is without sin, cast the first stone," (John 8:7).

Final Thoughts

We cannot justify sin. We cannot justify selfish decisions that are contrary to the Word of God. The quickest, sure-fire way to upend divine provision and purpose is to simply do things our way. When we truly expect greater things in our lives, we will seek God and, as Paul did, die to our flesh daily. Bottom line: if it goes against the Word of God, we shouldn't be doing it. Don't let justification of wrong decisions derail the plans God has for you.

Derailment #3: Listening to the Enemy/Unwise Counsel

I was five years old when my older brother convinced me to jump over the toy clock. We were in the basement of our house with one of Paul's friends, and they were taking turns running and jumping over this toy. They coerced me to participate. I ran and jumped and landed on my foot the wrong way. There was immediate pain, and I ended up with a broken ankle.

Now, I realize my brother was only eight years old at the time, and he wasn't trying to hurt me. However, he did not have the proper experience and understanding to pressure me to make that decision. He was having a good time with his buddy, and the two of them wanted me to experience it too. An adult would have observed what we were doing and would have determined that it was unsafe.

As the years progressed, many people came along, quick to give me advice. One time, I purchased a car I couldn't afford because I listened to a co-worker instead of my husband. My co-worker reasoned with me that I deserved a new car because I worked hard. My husband advised that I would struggle to make payments and to wait until I paid off other debt. But my flesh wanted the new car, so I decided that my co-worker's counsel was right. I jumped into a large car loan, and within months, I regretted it.

Who are you listening to? Those who we listen to influence our thought-processes and ultimately our decisions. Listening to the wrong counsel can adversely affect our decision-making process and ultimately our God-given dreams. Having a strong, spiritual mentor is important, as is making sure that anyone who counsels you is Spirit-filled and in right standing with God.

Red Flag #1: Murmuring and Complaining

There are red flags when listening to the counsel of others, and when it is not aligned with Scripture, it can deviate us from our God-directed path.

> *Blessed is the man who walketh not in the counsel of the ungodly, nor standeth in the way of sinners, nor sitteth in the seat of the scornful.*
> Psalm 1:1-1

If you want to be blessed, according to the above Scripture, you will use wisdom when choosing your friends and counsel. Think of the common cliché: misery loves company. There's a lot of truth in that statement. When we're upset, we like to find those who are upset too, or at least those who will listen to our agitation. Just like viruses, attitudes and perspectives are contagious. If we choose to hang around people who are miserable, angry, discontented, or jealous, then it will eventually affect us.

I've seen this firsthand in my own life, and not just in the car purchase. Several years back, a new family started attending our church. I really connected with them because they were from the downstate area and we knew many of the same people. It didn't take long for me to hang out with my new friend. I was already lonely, going through my own wilderness experience, and this woman was like a breath of fresh air in that regard. She was funny and bubbly, and a lot of fun to be around. It didn't take long for her to be unhappy with our church situation, and she was very vocal about it. Since I had become so close to her, I let her vent. Soon, my own issues with the church began to loom large in my mind. I started to be critical about everything. The church and its leadership couldn't do anything right. My friend and I would compare everything wrong with the church with the big churches we used to attend. When she and her family decided to attend another church, I began to question whether or not I wanted to stop going too.

My bad attitude and critical spirit began to rub off on my husband. He started to complain, and we would complain together, as our misery grew. We stepped away from ministry. Our attendance decreased to Sunday mornings only. Even then, we found excuses as to why we couldn't go.

This bitter and complaining spirit stayed with me for years. My friend and her family moved out of state, but her miserable attitude remained. When another family moved into the area, I was quick to make friends, and it didn't take long for my gossip and complaints about the church to resonate with them. My lightbulb moment came when they stopped coming. They didn't choose another church like my earlier friend's family did. Oh no, they simply stopped going to church. Their social media feed blew up with angry, sarcastic posts about the church in general.

When I saw this collateral damage that happened in large part because of me, conviction dropped me to my knees. My negativity led souls *away* from God instead of *to* Him. Even though I repented right then and apologized to the couple who stopped attending church, the damage had been done, and I still had my own bitter and complaining spirit to deal with. Just because we repent doesn't mean that all the negativity and baggage that's attached itself to us magically disappears. Satan isn't going to give up that easily. It takes a daily dying to the flesh and growing spiritually to completely break free from bondage.

If you are the one who is upset about something, go to the Lord first. Get your own heart right. If someone specifically has upset you, the Word says to go to *that person*. Do not undermine that person with gossip and discord because you then immediately take yourself outside of the will of God. I learned this important lesson the hard way.

Please, take heed. Complaining and gossiping are bad fruit that grow from the weed of bitterness and discontent. Jealousy also bears poisonous fruit. When you see these in others, gracefully remove yourself from that situation before you are affected. These bad apples of sin can derail you and push you outside the will of God. They have no place in a Christian's life.

Red Flag #2:
Worldly Advice

Everyone has an opinion, and now, with social media, most folks have a platform to voice their opinions. Even without social media and other forms of technology, we can find someone willing to give us advice.

Here's the rub: a lot of opinions are wrong. If they're not specifically wrong, they are often misguided and misdirected. Some will offer their opinions without us asking, but often, we go seeking someone to provide counsel.

Who do you go to?

Co-workers?

A close friend?

Your spouse?

King Rehobam is a Biblical example who learned the hard way about listening to the wrong counsel:

> *And king Rehoboam took counsel with the old men that had stood before Solomon his father while he yet lived, saying, What counsel give ye me to return answer to this people?*
>
> *And they spake unto him, saying, If thou be kind to this people, and please them, and speak good words to them, they will be thy servants forever.*
>
> *But he forsook the counsel which the old men gave him, and took counsel with the young men that were brought up with him, that stood before him.*
>
> *And he said unto them, What advice give ye*

> *that we may return answer to this people, which have spoken to me, saying, Ease somewhat the yoke that thy father did put upon us?*
> *And the young men that were brought up with him spake unto him, saying, Thus shalt thou answer the people that spake unto thee, saying, Thy father made our yoke heavy, but make thou it somewhat lighter for us; thus shalt thou say unto them, My little finger shall be thicker than my father's loins. For whereas my father put a heavy yoke upon you, I will put more to your yoke: my father chastised you with whips, but I will chastise you with scorpions.*
> 2 Chronicles 10:6-11

Rehoboam was the son of King Solomon and the grandson of King David. He took the throne after his father's death, and the Israelites rightly questioned how Rehoboam would reign. He approached the elders from his father's counsel, and they advised him to show the people kindness so that they would be loyal. His friends didn't agree. They advised for him to show the Israelites who was boss and to come down hard on them. Instead of listening to the wise counsel of the elders, he listened to his inexperienced friends. Because of this unwise decision, a rebellion grew and the kingdom of Israel and Judah was split, causing unnecessary conflict and discord.

Adam and Eve also made the unfortunate mistake of listening to unwise counsel. The unexpected consequences of their decision to listen to a voice who spoke against the Word of God not only cost them, but it had ramifications that affects us today:

> *Now the serpent was more subtle than any beast of the field which the Lord God had made.*
> *And he said unto the woman, Yea, hath God said, Ye shall not eat of every tree of the garden?*
> *And the woman said unto the serpent, We may eat of the fruit of the trees of the garden: But of the fruit of the tree which is in the midst of the garden, God hath said, Ye shall not eat of it, neither shall ye touch it, lest ye die.*
> *And the serpent said unto the woman, Ye shall not surely die.*
> *Genesis 3:1-4*

God Himself told them not to eat from the one tree. They received a command from the Lord, yet Eve chose to listen to a snake and Adam chose to listen to the woman. Both knew about God's directive, but what the serpent said was enticing. The serpent's words completely contradicted God's warning. Their decision cost humanity everything, separating us from God.

If we need counsel, the Bible couldn't be any clearer: Don't go to the ungodly. Who is the ungodly?

1. Anyone who does not have the spirit of Christ.
2. Anyone who contradicts the Word of God.

In Psalm 1:1, David wrote, "Blessed is the man who walketh not in the counsel of the ungodly, nor standeth in the way of sinners, nor sitteth in the seat of the scornful…" We are actually better off when we do not associate or listen to the ungodly, the negative, or the complainers. Misery *does* love company, and it behooves us to remember that surrounding ourselves with an echo chamber of those who have similar grievances is only going to derail the plan of God for us.

Final Thoughts

We need to be careful who we hang around and with who we listen to. Listening to the wrong people will have real ramifications in our walks with God and in aligning ourselves to His will.

Derailment #4: Going against His Word

God's will is His Word.

Read that again. Recite it until it gets in deep in your heart. He's not going to deviate from that. Ever.

God is not going to change His mind to fit our agendas.

But God, I love him. What's so wrong with living together?

I know I'm not supposed to gossip, but that person deserves what's coming to her.

So what that I have to lie to get ahead. God wouldn't have given me this ambition if He didn't want me to use it!

Nothing derails God's expectations for our dreams and goals more than making and justifying a decision outside of His will or before it is time. Many Christians will use popular phrases, such as "I feel God is leading me to do this..." or "God spoke to me and told me to do this..." If we are not careful, our selfish desires will trick us into thinking God approves, when in reality, we are only justifying our own will.

I have an acquaintance who is adamant that God told him he was going to receive a large inheritance once a certain relative died. God supposedly gave him a word to be patient and wait for it. While my acquaintance is waiting, he's not working. He lives on government assistance and routinely visits local food banks for groceries.

There's nothing necessarily wrong with this if he is unable to work. Many people need the assistance, and we should do what we can to help others. However, this man is able-bodied. He just doesn't want to work. He says that it's a test to see if he will continue to be patient and wait on the Lord. Just a side note: it's funny how we will often twist Scripture to fit our designs.

When asked about the Bible verses that clearly state that if a man will not work, he will not eat, or the servant who buried his talent and was cast into the lake of fire for being lazy, my acquaintance shakes his head and repeats, "I know what God told me."

Are we sure it's God speaking to us, or is it our flesh? How do we know? Because…wait for it…*God's will is His Word.* If a decision we have made goes against what the Bible says, then we, my friends, are outside of God's will. God not only won't bless the situation, He *can't* bless it. Nothing stops God's anointing faster than disobedience and an unrepentant heart.

When God Speaks…

First of all, His Word is final and unchanging. "The grass withereth, the flower fadeth: but the word of our God shall stand forever," (Isaiah 40:8). When Jesus commanded the seas to be calm, the waters obeyed (Mark 4:39). When He commanded the legion of demons out of the man from Gaderenes, the legion obeyed (Mark 5:1-20). When He told Lazarus to come out of the tomb, that's exactly what happened (John 11:43-44).

I'm not saying that through our prayers, God can't change

His mind or be moved by our requests. Look at what happened to Hezekiah in Isaiah 38. God sent the prophet to the sick king: "Thus saith the Lord, Set thine house in order: for thou shalt die, and not live." King Hezekiah prayed and asked God to deliver him. The prophet returned to Hezekiah and said, "Thus saith the Lord, the God of David thy father, I have heard thy prayer, I have seen thy tears: behold, I will add unto thy days fifteen years."

In another example, God was willing to spare Sodom and Gomorrah because Abraham asked him to do so. Over and over, Abraham pleaded with God, and God listened to his plea and agreed to spare the cities if only ten people were righteous. Unfortunately, not even ten were counted as righteous, and the cities were not spared. However, God did save Lot and his family because of Abraham's request (Genesis 18 & 19).

So yes, our prayers move heaven. And of course, God is compassionate—the Bible says His compassion fails not—and His will is for our good (Lamentations 3:22). What I am saying is once He speaks, it's final. Those words don't come back to Him void (Isaiah 55:11). And when He speaks, it's expected that we obey.

We live in a society where we want our ears tickled. We search for a church that will align with our ideals and philosophies. We say we believe in Jesus, but have we read and applied the Word? If and when we disobey God, we step outside of His will and presence. King Saul did just that. The prophet, Samuel, rebuked King Saul: "Hath the LORD as great delight in burnt offerings and sacrifices, as in obeying the voice of the LORD? Behold, to obey is better than sacrifice, and to hearken than the fat of rams," (I Samuel 15:22). His disobedience led to God removing the anointing and placing it upon David. Then there's Samson. His disobedience and disregard for his covenant with God led to God stripping him of divine power and ability. Even Moses, who was blessed mightily by God and who is still considered one of the greatest Godly leaders of all time, endured a consequence for disobeying God's direction and allowing one moment of anger to consume him.

What then is God's Word? The Bible is a pretty thick book, but for us to be aligned to it, we need to actually read it for ourselves. All of it is relevant not only for historical purposes, but also to see God's relationship with mankind since the very beginning. It opens our eyes to His desire for friendship and intimacy with His creation, and that it cannot happen when sin is present, not because God has this mile-long list of restrictions "just because." Oh no, God and sin simply don't mix.

When We Don't Listen...

Since Adam and Eve's decision to eat the fruit and sever the relationship between God and man, God has continually and consistently moved toward reconciliation. He doesn't want to be apart from us. He doesn't want us to suffer eternal consequences that were never meant for us.

Free will gives us the choice to listen and obey or to do our own thing. Word of warning: it never fares too well when we choose the latter.

> *Now the word of the Lord came unto Jonah the son of Amittai, saying, Arise, go to Nineveh, that great city, and cry against it;*

> *for their wickedness is come up before me. But Jonah rose up to flee unto Tarshish from the presence of the Lord, and went down to Joppa; and he found a ship going to Tarshish: so he paid the fare thereof, and went down into it, to go with them unto Tarshish from the presence of the Lord.*
> *But the Lord sent out a great wind into the sea, and there was a mighty tempest in the sea, so that the ship was like to be broken.*
> *Jonah 1: 1-4*

Oh Jonah, I feel your pain. God directed you to do something outside of your comfort zone. Instead of following God's plan, you decided to go in another direction. I can't even imagine what it felt like to be thrown overboard into an angry sea or the darkness that overtook you for three days and nights in the belly of a big fish. I don't want to imagine the smell and sensation of being fish puke.

Jonah's lesson is one for all of us. Going our own way and doing our own thing only causes more chaos and unnecessary obstacles than simply humbling ourselves before the Lord and obeying His Word. We'll be much better for it, and hopefully, avoid smelling like fish guts in the process.

Final Thoughts

The Bible provides clear directions for making sure we are following God's will, which is His Word. Anything that goes against the Word of God is out of alignment with His will. As stated in previous chapters, justifying our wrong decisions doesn't trick God into seeing things our way. His Word is a lamp unto our feet (Psalm 119:105), which means that it guides us on life's journey. Without it, we are stumbling blindly in the dark and derailing or delaying God's plans to come to fruition.

Derailment #5: Giving Up

I don't like to quit, but I can't say I never have. It goes against my grain to give up before the expected end, but that doesn't mean it doesn't happen from time to time. Just last week, my family and I visited Elk's Knob in North Carolina. It's a mountainous hike with a beautiful view. I hadn't practiced or hiked before. Ever. I didn't wear the right shoes, and we walked a one-mile trail before we found the upward trail that led to Elk's Knob. Unfortunately, I didn't make it. My sons did. They went on without me, and my poor husband stayed with me to make sure I got down the mountain's trail without hurting myself even more. I was sore for days, but it bugged me that I couldn't make it to the top.

When it comes to eating right and exercising, I know that doing so will produce healthy, positive results. But I have often given up before I reach the desired goal.

I don't enjoy the feeling that often follows, which is a feeling of defeat and disappointment.

When it comes to God's plan for our lives, many times we give up too soon. This generally comes from discouragement. Just because we have a God-given dream doesn't mean that it is going to follow our timeline. Peter and Judas are two examples of men who chose different paths for their lives. One allowed God to use him, and because of that, changed the world. The other one quit.

Peter Kept the Faith

He asked a lot of questions, but he also loved Jesus fiercely, so much so that he attacked a soldier and cut off his ear in an attempt to protect Jesus from being arrested. One would think that out of any of the disciples, Peter wouldn't be the one to deny Him, but that's exactly what he did.

> *Now Peter sat without in the palace: and a damsel came unto him, saying, Thou also wast with Jesus of Galilee. But he denied before them all, saying, I know not what thou sayest.*
> *And when he was gone out into the porch, another maid saw him, and said unto them that were there, This fellow was also with Jesus of Nazareth. And again he denied with an oath, I do not know the man.*
> *And after a while came unto him they that stood by, and said to Peter, Surely thou also art one of them; for thy speech bewrayeth thee. Then began he to curse and to swear, saying, I know not the man.*
> *And immediately the cock crew.*
> *And Peter remembered the word of Jesus, which said unto him, Before the cock crow, thou shalt deny me thrice. And he went out,*

and wept bitterly.
Matthew 26:69-74

Peter had some memorable moments with Jesus, including walking on water. He didn't want to believe it when Jesus told him that he would deny Jesus three times before the rooster crowed. In that moment, Peter realized what he had done. Here his friend, Jesus, whose revelation Peter believed, was suffering and sentenced to die in the hands of an angry mob, and Peter denied him to others. It's a heartbreaking story. I understand why he wept bitterly.

Thankfully, the story doesn't end there. After Jesus's death, Peter ran with John to verify the women's account that the grave was empty. He spent 40 days with the resurrected Jesus. I wonder what conversation they had. I wonder what Peter said to Jesus, or what Jesus said that would propel Peter to shake off the shame of his failure and instead shake the world with the gospel of truth. Peter was in the upper room in Acts 2 and received the Holy Spirit in a supernatural way, and it was Peter who preached to the crowd of thousands to "...repent, and be baptized, everyone of you, in the name of Jesus Christ, for the remission of sins, and ye shall receive the gift of the Holy Ghost," (Acts 2:38). It was Peter who preached to Cornelius and his household, showing the world that the Gospel message is for everyone, not just the Jews.

What would have happened if Peter's failures during Jesus's crucifixion caused him to quit? If he let the shame and bitter tears turn to actual bitterness? God's purpose for his life would not have been fulfilled. Peter showed the world the powerful message of not letting our failures define us.

Judas Gave Up

Judas Iscariot walked with Jesus too. He was one of the twelve disciples, a front row observer of the miracles, with a front row seat to Jesus's sermons, but for thirty pieces of silver, he betrayed his friend. Even when Jesus called him out on it, Judas still went through with his plan. What led to Judas's decision? We may never know, but before I judge him, I have to question how many times I've betrayed my Savior. How many times has the pull of the world led me to sell the truth in exchange for a lie? In all honesty, I can't judge Judas because I'm a sinner too. But I can examine his actions and learn from them. One thing I've learned from all of this is that Judas quit too soon.

> *Then Judas, which had betrayed him, when he saw that he was condemned, repented himself, and brought again the thirty pieces of silver to the chief priests and elders, Saying, I have sinned in that I have betrayed the innocent blood. And they said, What is that to us? see thou to that. And he cast down the pieces of silver in the temple, and departed, and went and hanged himself. Matthew 27: 3-5*

The same forgiveness that applied to Peter was also available to Judas, but Judas allowed the guilt and shame to lead to his demise. His actions were deplorable, yet Jesus died for Judas too. What would have been Judas's testimony if he hadn't given in to the darkness? Unfortunately, we will never know. Judas gave up, which halted God's expectations for his life. In these examples, both made mistakes, but one chose to keep walking in the faith and went on to preach the Gospel, while the other one quit. Let us heed this lesson in our own lives.

Giving Up Affects Others

Why is giving up such a travesty? From earlier chapters we know that God expects us to be kingdom-minded. His plan is always more than just us. When we give up, we derail not only the blessings and promises God has for us, but our decision negatively affects others. God's purpose is not only for *your* good, but it's also for the *greater* good.

First, there's giving up earthly goals and dreams. Let's say you enroll in college to earn a degree to improve your career. That's an earthly goal, but it can also have greater good. Your family will be blessed by your completion. Your church may be blessed by larger offering and tithe contributions. Your growth in study and academics could bless other areas of your life. If you quit college, then that decision doesn't just affect you. It affects those around you. That said, there are some earthly goals that we put in front of us that may not be God-ordained and can lead us off onto a wrong path, a path that God never intended for us to walk on. It's important to have goals, but we need to make sure that they are aligned to God's Word and His plan.

There are also spiritual goals and dreams. Quitting could cause massive damage to your soul and the souls of others. We should all have the spiritual goal to draw closer to the Lord. What if we quit? What if we decide that serving the Lord is too much? What—or who—will be the collateral damage?

I know a man who grew up in the church, dated a girl from college, brought her to the Lord, and eventually got married, and had a beautiful family. The man became disillusioned by several aspects of the church, and for whatever reason, stopped coming. It wasn't that he necessarily turned to a "life of sin," he simply decided that he didn't need to attend church to be saved. Soon, the disillusionment turned to bitterness. His wife still came to church with their children, but he was ugly about it. I remember counseling her on several occasions, encouraging her to keep the faith, but it became too much for her. After nearly two years of trying to come to church with the kids while dealing with an angry and bitter husband, the woman stopped coming too. When the kids were tweens, the man had an epiphany and came back to the Lord. His kids would come with him on occasion, but never his wife. She wanted nothing to do with it and labeled herself agnostic. The man has said repeatedly that he feels he will have to answer for his wrong decision in leading his family away from God.

This situation breaks my heart, and how much more so is the Lord grieved by it? Our decisions matter. They matter to a lot of people. The decision to quit not only derails God's purpose for our lives, but it has long-lasting consequences to those who look to us.

Final Thoughts

Becoming discouraged happens to all of us, but it is important to not let failure, disillusionment, or closed doors lead to quitting. God's will for our lives can't be fulfilled when we give up. Not only can God's will be hindered, but we could also negatively affect others. Paul warns that we are to be careful, so as not to be a stumbling block to someone else (I Corinthians 8:9).

Derailment #6: Getting Offended

Our family moved to Cadillac, Michigan, in 2013. We were coming from another Northern Michigan town, and John and I were tired and burned out in a lot ways. We made the conscientious decision to not hold grudges, but to start fresh. This included trying to find the right church for us.

There are not big churches in Northern Michigan, especially Pentecostal churches, but we found a small church with a sweet little congregation. The pastor and his wife were thrilled when they found out I was a teacher, and I was more than willing to jump into their small Sunday School program. Within our first year, they asked me to take the helm of morning Sunday School for the children between 4 and 12 years old. We decided having a children's church format would work well since we didn't have enough teachers. God was in it, and it didn't take long for children to start attending. Neighborhood children would walk in on their own, grandchildren of attendees started to show up regularly, and new families liked the program so much that they made the church their home. By the end of that first year, the little Sunday morning children's church was running close to 20 children, and sometimes we were over 20 kids. I worked with a few faithful folks to put together a Vacation Bible School, and it was a huge success. Close to 30 children attended all three evenings, and the Sunday service that followed was powerful.

But then there was a shift.

The pastor's wife had a friend who started coming, and she wanted to be a Sunday School teacher. Great! I was thrilled. The only help I had in the children's church was my teenage son. But there was a caveat. She didn't want to work with me in the children's church. She wanted her own class. When the pastor's wife approached me that they were taking Sunday School in a different direction, I begged her to reconsider. What we were doing was working! Almost half our church was children, and they were coming because they loved Sunday School. She agreed, or so I thought.

Two months later I received a text that the next Sunday there would be a new format. They were splitting the ages.

I felt like my heart had been trampled. Not for glory or pride, oh no, my heart was—and is always—for the children. I knew the kids would be devastated. I sobbed, but I shook myself and went to church with a smile on my face. The kids would look to me, and I wanted to be strong and loving, even if the situation was handled horribly by the others.

It hurts me to even write these next words. The children were, in fact, devastated. The younger ones who were being forced to leave threw themselves on me, begging to stay (Remember, most of these children were from the neighborhood, and not from "church homes.") There were tears and tantrums. Parents came to see what all the fuss was about (these were the new parents), and they too became agitated. I asked the pastor's wife privately to let them adjust, but I was quickly shot down and told that they'd take it better if I told them that this is what needed to be done.

My heart was broken, and in all transparency, it never fully recovered. The Sunday School program, even with my continued efforts in the one class, lost half the children. My class, which was once close to 20 students, went to five on a good Sunday, and all five of them were from church regulars. The new families stopped coming, and I never once heard an apology from the pastor's wife or her friend.

I shared that story to share this important piece of information: *I was offended.* Not only was I offended, I was hurt and angry. If I would have had my way, I would have left the church immediately. But John didn't want to church shop on account of my offense. Even though he grieved with me, and was just as upset over the situation, he made the decision to stay, and so I submitted.

But, oh, how I stewed.

I watched in horror as the church went from running around 80 to not even coming close to 30 attendees.

I couldn't stay offended. My heart remained steadfast, and it was toward the children. I gave my all and continued field trips and Sunday School outings. We'd have a sledding Saturday, and a yearly trip to the pumpkin patch, but I had to constantly wrestle with my flesh to not let my offense pull me from the children's ministry. Even if only a handful of children came, I would teach and love those few. It took a continual swallowing down of the offense I still felt in my heart.

The Problem with Offense

If someone causes an offense, that person violated a moral rule or transgressed against someone else. To *take offense* is different. When we are offended, we are hurt and/or angry by the actions or words of another person. There is not much we can do when it comes to other people's words or actions. However, we can determine how we will act in such a circumstance.

Let's be honest. There are times when people can be hurtful. Maybe it's intentional, maybe it's not, but insensitivity and tactlessness have existed through the ages. I've been on the receiving end of hurtful words and offensive situations. I get it. It can be infuriating, and the enemy knows this.

The enemy knows that if he can get us focused on the perceived hurt, then our eyes will turn away from God. Before long, the issue that was so offensive looms large. A few things could happen:

1. We could make an impulsive, emotional decision that has lasting consequences.
2. We could grumble and complain to anyone willing to listen, sowing seeds of discord.
3. We could retaliate.
4. We could dwell on it.

In any of these scenarios, the offense can derail the fulfillment of God's purpose in our lives. In complete transparency, it's a sin to harbor ill-will toward anyone. Forgiveness is a requirement, and healing only comes when there is forgiveness. Unfortunately, I've observed this numerous times, both inside and outside the church. Friendships have been ripped apart because of a perceived offense. Families have left the church because of offense. Individuals have actually walked away from the Lord because of hurt and offense.

The Pharisees were the religious elite, and they constantly were offended. Offense is another way to derail God's expectations for our lives. Offense leads to bitterness and unforgiveness. It is difficult to walk in the will of God when you are harboring bitterness or unforgiveness due to someone's perceived insult or actions. When we are offended, it is our ego that is bothered, and our ego is a manifestation of pride.

There is a spirit of offense, and if we're not careful, we will find ourselves struggling with offense in several areas. Being offended leads to becoming critical, and then we start complaining. Offense and complaints are two bedfellows with potent ramifications. They're like heavy weights tied around our ankles that keep us from moving forward in life.

Why is this?

When we are offended, we're no longer focused on God. When we are offended, we make impulsive decisions. These decisions could be to get back at another person or to walk away from the divine path in order to prove a point. Holding onto offense, however, causes more than derailing our divine destinies. It has eternal consequences. How so? In Matthew 18, Peter asks Jesus, "Lord, how oft shall my brother sin against me, and I forgive him? Till seven times?" Basically Peter is asking Jesus what to do with repeated offenses. Jesus tells him that he needs to forgive "seventy times seven," but provides a parable that explains what happens if we don't let go:

> *Therefore is the kingdom of heaven likened unto a certain king, which would take account of his servants. And when he had begun to reckon, one was brought unto him, which owed him ten thousand talents. But forasmuch as he had not to pay, his lord commanded him to be sold, and his wife, and children, and all that he had, and payment to be made. The servant therefore fell down, and worshipped him, saying, Lord, have patience with me, and I will pay thee all. Then the lord of that servant was moved with compassion, and loosed him, and forgave him the debt. But the same servant went out, and found one of his fellowservants, which owed him an hundred pence: and he laid hands on him, and took him by the throat, saying, Pay me that thou owest. And his fellowservant fell down at his feet, and besought him, saying, Have patience with me, and I will pay thee all. And he would not: but went and cast him into prison, till he should pay the debt. So when his fellowservants saw what was done, they were very sorry, and came and told unto their lord all that was done. Then his lord, after that he had called him, said unto him, O thou wicked servant, I forgave thee*

all that debt, because thou desiredst me: Shouldest not thou also have had compassion on thy fellowservant, even as I had pity on thee? And his lord was wroth, and delivered him to the tormentors, till he should pay all that was due unto him. So likewise shall my heavenly Father do also unto you, if ye from your hearts forgive not everyone his brother their trespasses.
Matthew 18: 23-35

Jesus didn't mince words when it came to getting offended:

Woe unto the world because of offences! for it must needs be that offences come; but woe to that man by whom the offence cometh! Wherefore if thy hand or thy foot offend thee, cut them off, and cast them from thee: it is better for thee to enter into life halt or maimed, rather than having two hands or two feet to be cast into everlasting fire. And if thine eye offend thee, pluck it out, and cast it from thee: it is better for thee to enter into life with one eye, rather than having two eyes to be cast into hell fire.
Matthew 18: 7-9

Final Thoughts

Getting offended and staying offended can be a major stumbling block for every believer. We have to let it go. Not so much for anyone else's sake but for our own.

But it's so hard!
You don't know what they did to me!
You don't know what was said about me!
You don't know what happened!

No, I don't know, but God does, and He still wants us to let it go.

It's God's desire for us to live peacefully with all men. There aren't any contingencies for getting out of that. Don't let offense derail God's plan for you. More so, don't let it keep you from heaven.

Derailment #7: Blaming Others

"Mom! Bobby won't stop poking me!"
"Yeah, but Suzie punched me!"
"Don't tattle! I don't want to hear it!"

How many times did we hear similar words when we were children? How many times have we said that to our own children? Tattling is annoying most of the time because it's often trivial and immature. When children tattle, they point a finger at the person doing the offense. Unfortunately, the need to tattle doesn't really go away. It merely morphs into the blame game.

Blaming is when we remove ourselves from any ownership of a situation or action and instead place it at the feet of someone else. Blaming also involves deflecting to keep others from looking at us as the cause or part of a problem. Aaron quickly blamed the children of Israel for the golden calf incident: "And Aaron said, Let not the anger of my lord wax hot: thou knowest the people, that they are set on mischief," (Exodus 32:22).

Refusing ownership for our own bad actions shows immaturity and carnality. God can't heal when we refuse the help. The power of accepting one's own culpability is that doing so allows us to place our sins and imperfections at the foot of the cross. We're not able to do that if we are too busy pointing a finger at others.

Understanding the 'Why'

Why do we blame others? The answer seems simple. It's easier to see the fault in other people, yet the answer is a lot more complex.

1. **We have become gods in our own minds and hearts.**

    In 2 Timothy 3:2, it says, "For men shall be lovers of their own selves, covetous, boasters, proud, blasphemers, disobedient to parents, unthankful, unholy." We love ourselves so much that we have become proud and boastful. Even children and young people display this by disrespecting authority and talking back to parents and elders. Why listen to others when we know it all ourselves?

    Think of how we respond to criticism or anyone who dares give us advice. How dare they! Don't tell me how to raise my kids. Don't tell me how to live my life. Don't tell me what to do. No one asked you. This way of thinking leads to ramifications in our lives and in future generations, and it ultimately stops God from working in our lives because we have become our own gods. By esteeming ourselves above God and others, our first reaction when confronted with criticism or anything that raises awareness to a deficit on our part is to become defensive and deflect.

2. **Our worldly culture of hedonism and self-centeredness has rubbed off on us.**

    In 2 Corinthians 6:17, Paul admonishes us to "come out from among them, and be ye separate," yet the secularism of the culture has rubbed off on us. Standards have slipped so much that it's hard to distinguish the Christians from the world. The blame game begins as we start spouting all the reasons for this blurring of the lines.

3. **We don't want to change.**

    Change is uncomfortable. It's easier to see another person's faults or culpability in a situation than to examine ourselves.

4. **We have embraced the 'victim' mindset.**

    When we blame others, we fail to see the problems with our own actions.

Seeing Our Own Faults

John and I are approaching our 25th wedding anniversary, and the years have definitely had some ups and downs. Several years back, one of our mutual friends were in the process of a divorce. He asked John, "How do you and Janice make it work? You make it look so easy!" John quickly replied that there was nothing easy to it. Marriage takes hard work. Every day. Part of that hard work comes from communication and an openness to work on yourself.

During our early years of marriage, there was a lot of the blame game happening. We'd get into an argument, and it would only escalate because neither one of us would admit our own culpability in the problem. We easily saw the faults in each other!

Think of your current circles of relationship: family, spouse, career, community groups, friends, etc. Now think of some issues or challenges that these different groups deal with on a consistent basis. Ask yourself this: What are your contributions to this issue/challenge? Are you adding to the challenge by complaining, pointing fingers, gossiping, manipulating others to see it your way, etc.? Or, are you alleviating the challenge by trying to find solutions, listening to others, remaining positive, praying for resolution, speaking peace, etc.?

How we approach the relationships in our lives is similar to how we approach God. Are we quick to complain, finding fault in everything but ourselves? Or, even worse, are we blaming God for issues/challenges, completely blind to our own culpability? In 1 John 1:9, it reads, "If we confess our sins, he is faithful and just to forgive us our sins, and to cleanse us from all unrighteousness."

The first step is confession. Seeing our own faults is paramount to fulfilling God's purpose in our lives because if we cannot see or confess our own issues, then we are holding onto sin. Sin and God cannot mix. King Solomon shared similar sentiments in Proverbs 28:13: "He that covereth his sins shall not prosper: but whoso confesseth and forsaketh them shall have mercy."

Final Thoughts

Blaming others is another way to sabotage God's will in our lives. When we blame others, we refuse repentance of our own wrongdoings, as well as hold on to grudges and unforgiveness. In the Biblical example of Job, we see a man who could have easily blamed God and other people for the horrible events in his life, yet he chose not play the blame game. The blessings of the Lord were restored to him several times over because of his faithfulness to God and his unwillingness to become a bitter fault-finder.

If we are expecting God to perform the miraculous in our lives, or if we are expecting His promise to come to fruition, we must be willing to examine ourselves and be open to growing in Christ. Refusal to admit mistakes is a refusal to repent. An unrepentant heart is an unmalleable heart, and God can't work in our lives if we are too hardened to be molded to His will.

Part III: Pursuing God's Expectations

Godly Pursuit #1: Tap into His Power

When we walk through the door of our homes and flip the light switch, we probably don't stop to even think about—let alone appreciate—the miracle of harnessed electricity. It's in our everyday lives, so much so that when we lose power, we become immediately aware of the inconvenience. The power of electricity is not in the light switches of our homes, but the power is transferred from a source, often a city or township power grid.

In much the same way, we are powerless without tapping into the power source. Some may find the previous sentence arguable, and maybe even a little insulting.

I'm not powerless!
I'm in control of my life!
I do what I want to do!
No one orders me around!

If we stop and think about it, how "in control" are we? If I'm honest with myself, I am not in control of anything outside of my thoughts and actions. My mother would tell me, "You are not responsible for other people's words or actions, but you are responsible for your own." Basically, I don't have any control over anything outside of myself. So, let me urge you to be careful with this type of thinking. In order to tap into

God's power, we have to humbly acknowledge that without God, we are nothing.

Beware of Counterfeit Power

It's human nature to not only survive, but to thrive. It's why we have so many modern-day conveniences. There is a certain feeling of power that comes with this. We feel powerful when we are thriving. For example, let's say we make a series of decisions that ultimately lead to a job promotion or an increase in prestige and influence. If we're not careful, we may become prideful at our decisions leading to such results. But these results and the feelings that come with it are superficial and fleeting. It's this false sense of power that can be dangerous because it leads to pride.

Counterfeit power is manipulative and arrogant. It reminds me of the scene from the Disney/Pixar movie, *A Bug's Life*. The grasshoppers are enjoying themselves at their local establishment, and one of the grasshoppers mentions to Hopper, the leader, why they can't just leave the ants alone and keep enjoying themselves. Hopper's words went something like this: "Those puny little ants outnumber us a hundred to one and if they ever figure that out there goes our way of life! It's not about food, it's about keeping those ants in line."

Counterfeit power seeks our own desires, even at the expense of others.

Counterfeit power feeds pride.

Counterfeit power lies to us, telling us that we are "in charge."

Counterfeit power elevates us to positions of platform and

prestige while separating us from those who have not "arrived."

Remember that everything with the enemy is a counterfeit to God's true design. Relying on ourselves is the root of secular humanism. In secular humanism, there is no need for God in our lives. We are capable of morality without Him. This nonreligious viewpoint gives humans this counterfeit power. These individuals deride the notion that we are not powerful.

Let's be real, mankind has accomplished some pretty amazing things. It's hard not to pat our own backs. Look what happened in Genesis 11. Humanity came together under one language and decided to build a tower that would ascend into the heavens. At first, they were successful.

And the Lord came down to see the city and the tower, which the children of men builded. And the Lord said, Behold, the people is one, and they have all one language; and this they begin to do: and now nothing will be restrained from them, which they have imagined to do. Go to, let us go down, and there confound their language, that they may not understand one another's speech. So the Lord scattered them abroad from thence upon the face of all the earth: and they left off to build the city. Therefore is the name of it called Babel; because the Lord did there confound the language of all the earth: and from

thence did the Lord scatter them abroad upon the face of all the earth.
Genesis 11: 5-9

This Biblical example shows that all of our manmade accomplishments are a result of God's blessings. They can also be taken away just as swiftly. In Job 1:21, it says, "Naked came I out of my mother's womb, and naked shall I return thither: the LORD gave, and the LORD hath taken away; blessed be the name of the LORD."

Euphemisms like "I've got this," or "I rely on no one but myself," or even "Anything you can do, I can do better," may all seem like encouraging or inspirational phrases. This type of thinking is the opposite of tapping into the divine's power. Paul said, "Oh, wretched man that I am! Who shall deliver me from the body of this death…So then with the mind I myself serve the law of God; but with the flesh the law of sin," (Romans 7:24-25). In the same chapter of Romans, Paul wrote, "For I know that in me (that is, in my flesh,) dwelleth no good thing: for to will is present with me; but how to perform that which is good I find not."

I can try to influence a situation or manipulate it somehow, but in all reality, control is a myth. Let's recognize counterfeit power for what it is. It is a cheap, watered-down, off-brand bogus imitation of the original.

God's Power Can Be Ours

More times than not, I don't feel too powerful. When things happen outside my control or influence, it produces anxiety. I've never been an anxious person, per se, but I recently experienced anxiety and what the doctor described as panic attacks. When the coronavirus pandemic hit the United States, I shrugged it off. At first. Then, in what seemed like the snap of someone's fingers, the economy halted. Schools were shut down. We were forced to stay home under lockdown orders. Churches were closed.

Within a couple days' time, I was working from home, as was my twelve-year-old son, Benjamin, and my main socialization—my church family and my extended family—halted. I had to quickly navigate Ben's schooling while navigating the college classes for my own students. I began to suffer from horrible insomnia. In my forty-six years on this earth, I've never struggled with sleep like I did in March and April of 2020. I'd lie in bed with my heart racing. The clock would move one hour, then another, then another. I'd get up and try sleeping on one couch, then I'd get up and try sleeping in another room with the futon, and then around six in the morning, I'd give up and go make coffee. But that was happening night after night. I'd occasionally fall asleep around 7 a.m. and my body would jolt awake around 10 a.m. I can't even describe my misery. In those lonely, late night hours, I would sob. I begged God to deliver me. When the doctor prescribed medicine for anxiety, I didn't even hesitate to take it. I wasn't proud. If it helped, I wanted it. Only, it didn't help.

In that desperation, I resorted to prayer and fasting. I've always been a praying woman—and I say that with humility—just like my mom. However, I've never been a fasting kind of woman. I don't mind fasting media or other technologies, but I like food. Don't ask me to give it up, especially coffee. But one night around five in the morning, I offered God my everything. I was finally willing to sacrifice it all. The fast was simple. Nothing with calories until 5 p.m. The fast would last until I experienced a breakthrough. The first day was miserable. I was already mentally and physically exhausted, but now I could add hungry and cranky to my list of miserable symptoms. But I needed God's intervention more than I needed anything else. I was determined.

My prayers increased as one day turned into another. I refused to accept anything other than complete restoration of my sleep. It didn't take long for my prayers to shift. Instead of praying for deliverance from insomnia, I began to pray for peace and for a sound mind. I began to change my focus from myself to others. My sister needed healing for a blood clot. My niece needed God's touch for a major surgery. My older son needed direction in his life regarding a specific situation. Friends needed healing. And then it happened.

I went to bed, closed my eyes, and fell asleep. I slept the entire night, and then the next night, and then the next. And I'm not talking restless sleep where I'd toss a turn and get a few hours here and there. I'm talking my head hit the pillow, and I slept until it was time to get up. Interestingly, I can't tell you how long I fasted. I know it was over a week, but it was because a shift happened in my walk with God. I changed focus. When I got my eyes off of myself and my situation, I was able to tap into God's divine power.

The fact is, "Every good and every perfect gift is from above, and cometh down from the Father of lights, with whom is no variableness, neither shadow of turning," (James 1:17). True power comes when we realize our fallibility and powerlessness. How can that be? When we recognize it's not who we are, but it's who HE is, we humble ourselves and allow a clear path for God's power to manifest in our lives.

Paul and Silas

> *And the multitude rose up together against them: and the magistrates rent off their clothes, and commanded to beat them. And when they had laid many stripes upon them, they cast them into prison, charging the jailor to keep them safely: Who, having received such a charge, thrust them into the inner prison, and made their feet fast in the stocks. And at midnight Paul and Silas prayed, and sang praises unto God: and the prisoners heard them. And suddenly there was a great earthquake, so that the foundations of the prison were shaken: and immediately all the doors were opened, and every one's bands were loosed. Acts 16:22-26*

Paul and Silas were in ministry. They were proclaiming the Gospel. This resulted in a crowd rising against them (Isn't it interesting how angry people become when the truth is presented?), and beating them before throwing them in prison. Consider the situation. How many of us would be upset at God's lack of protection?

Where are you, God?

Here I am, doing your work, and you can't even protect me from the enemy?

Instead of asking these questions, Paul and Silas made a decision to tap into the divine power source.

If you want to get God's attention, stop complaining and start worshiping. And that's exactly what Paul and Silas did. Nowhere in these verses does it say that they begged for God to deliver them.

1. **We must be infilled with His power.**

    "And ye shall be filled with power after that the Holy Ghost is come upon you…" (Acts 1:8).

    Without the Holy Ghost dwelling inside of us, we are truly powerless. But when we receive His Spirit (as evidenced in Acts chapter 2), then "Greater is He that is in [us], than he that is in the world," (1 John 4:4).

2. **Our focus needs to be set on Him.**

    Our help comes from Him, not the world. Psalm 121 speaks to this:

I will lift up mine eyes unto the hills, from whence cometh my help. My help cometh from the Lord, which made heaven and earth. He will not suffer thy foot to be moved: he that keepeth thee will not slumber. Behold, he that keepeth Israel shall neither slumber nor sleep. The Lord is thy keeper: the Lord is thy shade upon thy right hand. The sun shall not smite thee by day, nor the moon by night. The Lord shall preserve thee from all evil: he shall preserve thy soul. The Lord shall preserve

thy going out and thy coming in from this time forth, and even for evermore.
Psalm 121

---

3. **Worship through the trials.**

    As David exclaimed in Psalm 84:10, "For a day in thy courts is better than a thousand. I had rather be a doorkeeper in the house of my God, than to dwell in the tents of wickedness." There is no better place to be than in the presence of the Lord. Worship is our gateway into His presence. And "…in thy presence is fulness of joy; at thy right hand there are pleasures for evermore," (Psalm 16:11).

4. **Have faith and trust His process.**

    In Hebrews 11:6, it says, "But without faith, it is impossible to please Him: for he that cometh to God must believe that He is, and that He is a rewarder of them that diligently seek Him."

    Tapping into God's power starts by faith. Without faith, we block God's divine interventions in our lives. That's why the enemy's modus operandi is to get us to doubt and become worried or fearful. Fear robs us of faith.

5. **Prayer and fasting are a power-packed combo.**

    In Matthew 17, Jesus healed a little girl by rebuking the demon from her after the disciples had tried to heal her and failed. Naturally, the disciples asked Jesus what the secret to His success was. "Why could not we cast him out?" There were two parts to Jesus's answer. First, he admonishes them to have faith. "Because of your unbelief…If ye have faith as a grain of mustard seed, ye shall say unto this mountain, Remove hence to yonder place; and it shall remove; and nothing shall be impossible unto you." Jesus, however, wasn't finished with His answer. "Howbeit this kind goeth not out but by prayer and fasting," (Matthew 17: 19-21).

When we pray and fast, we are denying our flesh. God's divine power moves more freely when we are a willing vessel with a metaphoric crucified flesh. When we die to self, God's Spirit is no longer inhibited. I am a witness to this. In my own life, when I prayed and fasted, God performed the miraculous. It's important to note that we don't pray and fast in order to get God to *perform*, but when we die to ourselves and truly seek God, we are truly tapping into the supernatural.

6. **Put on the unmatchable armor of God**.

In Ephesians 6:11, Paul admonishes us to "Put on the whole armor of God, that ye may be able to stand against the wiles of the devil." Verse 13 goes further to say that we need to have on the whole armor of God to "withstand in the evil day." These verses let us know a couple things. First, the devil is fighting against us by using whatever he can to attack us. These attacks can be personal, but they can also be global (affecting our families, our communities, our nation, our world). Verse 12 clarifies this: "For we wrestle not against flesh and blood, but against principalities, against powers, against the rulers of the darkness of this world, against spiritual wickedness in high places."

Ephesians 6:11 also gives us our best strategy to win against the enemy, and that's putting on the supernatural armor of God. Tapping into God's power means "...having your loins girt about with truth, and having on the breastplate of righteousness..." It means having "...your feet shod with the preparation of the gospel of peace...taking the shield of faith...and...the helmet of salvation, and the sword of the Spirit, which is the word of God," (Ephesians 6: 14-17).

I could write an entire book on the armor of God—and maybe at another time I will—but let me stress the need for a daily armor-of-God assembly. Without the armor of God, not only will we forfeit our access into divine power and authority, we will falter and fall.

Final Thoughts

The Bible says that God does not leave us comfortless. We are not in the battle alone, and pursuing His expectations for our lives means tapping into that power source in order to overcome. This means understanding we have an enemy, but we also have battle armor that is meant to protect from the fiery darts of the wicked. We have resources at our disposal to tap into God's power. When we pursue Him and put Him first, no weapon formed against us is going to prosper. Even more so, God's expectations will begin to manifest in our lives as our thoughts and plans begin to align with His.

So, are you fearful? Let go of it and tap into God's divine power.

Do you have questions? It's time to set those questions aside and tap into God's power source.

Are you discouraged? Angry? Depressed? Overwhelmed? Stop what you're doing. Stop harboring these negative feelings and reach out to God. It's time to strengthen yourself with God's power and authority.

Godly Pursuit #2: Take Time to Grow

From the time David was anointed to be king to the time he received the crown at Ziklag was around 18 years. From the time Joseph's brothers betrayed him to the time he rose to power in Egypt, it was approximately 13 years. Moses hid in the desert 40 years before God spoke to him through a burning bush. Joshua was around the age of 59 when he took Moses' position as Israel's leader.

My point?

Time.

We are so consumed with time, yet God is not. God created time, but He is not constrained by it like we are. This creates frustration in our lives, or at least it does in mine. It's as if my brain knows that I only have a set number of days to accomplish what needs to be done. We don't know what tomorrow holds, which can put a fire within us to stay motivated and keep pushing. When we hit a wall, and our plans come to a screeching halt, the seconds turn to minutes, then hours, days, months and years. Being frustrated is an understatement.

Sometimes we respond to time's limits with spontaneity or impulsive decisions. There's something to be said for being impulsive. Impulsivity can be fun and enthralling. My mom and dad would sometimes pack us kids in the car while camping up north and just go on road trips. We'd end up in different locations and stop to investigate before climbing in the station wagon (or in later years van) and seeing where the road took us next. However, impulsiveness in life's decisions, especially when we're making a rash move based on our emotions or immediate circumstances, doesn't always work out.

God doesn't make rash decisions. He has a plan, and His plans take time.

This is not to say that He doesn't do the miraculous suddenly. Of course, He does, but that might have been His plan all along. When it comes to our lives, God's in it for the long haul. He wants to be Lord of our lives, not just Lord in those moments when we're seeking the miraculous, but Lord in every moment. He sees what we cannot see. He knows what we do not. His understanding is far above ours. And often, we are not ready in a moment for His purpose to be fulfilled. In John 15:2, Jesus explains, "Every branch in me that beareth not fruit he taketh away: and every branch that beareth fruit, he purgeth it, that it may bring forth more fruit." This verse demonstrates the importance of time and process.

It takes time for any plant to bear fruit. I received a beautiful lilac bush for Mother's Day, and I immediately planted it, following the directions carefully. I gave it fertilized soil, and I watered it daily. It didn't take long for the blossoms to fade. I thought, *That's okay, I'll see them next year.* Only, the fragrant blooms didn't come back the next year. I was so disappointed. I thought I had done something wrong, but my mother encouraged me to keep watering and nurturing the plant. She said, "Sometimes it takes a couple years for anything newly planted to bloom." She was right. Every spring, for the next three years, the lilac bush would become green and vibrant, but it didn't bloom. Imagine my joy one spring morning when I spotted lilacs in my lilac bush! Life lesson learned. Most plants take time to grow. A seed gets planted, whether strategically or haphazardly, and over the course of seasons, that seed takes root, growing and blossoming.

Jesus also suggests the importance of process in our growth. He stated that if we bear fruit, God would actually prune us so that we can bear more fruit.

Joseph's Dreams

I've always connected with Joseph, mostly because I felt bad for him. His brothers were jerks, and Potiphar's wife was a conniving snake. Joseph was a dreamer, and he had these dreams where his family would bow down to him. Sure, that sounds cocky, but to conspire to kill him over it? That never sat right with me.

> *But as for you, ye thought evil against me; but God meant it unto good, to bring to pass, as it is this day, to save much people alive.*
> Genesis 50:20

Joseph went through years of mistreatment, others' deceptions, others' abuse of power, and he endured jealousy and punishment for things outside of his control. In all honesty, I have a hard time understanding God's purpose in Joseph's pain. Why send this poor guy to jail for a crime he didn't commit? Why have the butler forget about him for years? Why have Joseph's brothers get away with the horrible mistreatment?

Here's what we do know. We know that Joseph was preferred over the other brothers. He was spoiled, and the firstborn of Jacob's favorite wife, Rachel. We know what many of us would become if put into a position of favoritism and comfort, we would probably get used to it and take it for granted. We might even rub it in the others' faces. God obviously saw something in Joseph. Something that would allow him to lead a nation. He had to prepare him for greatness, and that meant humbling him. God placed Joseph in high favor in whatever situation he found himself in, but He also needed Joseph to rely only on Him. Joseph had to be stripped of power and any haughtiness that would make him stumble and think that it was his doing that led to his rise. Not only that, but God needed restoration and healing between Joseph and his brothers. This meant that Joseph would need to let go of whatever bitterness and hurt he felt all those years later.

That took time, thirteen years' worth of time.

From my limited understanding, I freely admit that growing in God takes time. I am a much different person than I was five, ten, or twenty years ago. By pursuing God first, I've allowed Him to work on me, even when it has been uncomfortable. What I often remind myself is that God doesn't lie, and that His promise to me will not return void. That means that if His purpose and plan for my life is to be fulfilled, then it will happen in His time. Not mine. Through

His open doors. Not mine.

Taking time to grow in Him has developed my love for Him and His Word in ways that are hard to explain. *I love Him.* I simply love Him. God is more than my Heavenly Father. He is my best friend. As the song says, He truly is my way maker, miracle worker, and promise keeper, and I am closer to Him now than I've ever been.

Final Thoughts

Would we give a baby a steak to eat? Just like with our natural children, God knows that we might not be ready for all that He has in store for us. However, some of us never become ready for His promises because we stay spiritually stagnant. Not only that, but growing in Christ means we know His voice and His word. I encourage you to continue to grow in Christ. To not become complacent in your walk with God, but to continually keep Him as Lord of your lives.

Take the time to grow in Him. Don't become impatient. Don't make rash decisions. Trust Him. Lean on Him. Strengthen your relationship with Him.

He won't let you down. Don't just take my word for it…take His.

> *"Whatsoever things are true, whatsoever things are honest, whatsoever things are just, whatsoever things are pure, whatsoever things are lovely, whatsoever things are of a good report; if there be any virtue, and if there be any praise, think on these things."*
> *Philippians 4:8*

Godly Pursuit #3: Take Out the Trash

My brother had the chore of taking out the trash, and he hated it. He'd wait for the trash to be overflowing. Mom would yell at him, "Billy Paul! Take out this trash right now!" Being the good sister I am, I'd help him out by pushing the trash down as much as I could to give him a little more time before he'd have to take it out.

Now I see my own sons do the same trick. I've caught them pushing the trash down further into the garbage bag to give them some extra time before they have to lug the stinky bag outside to the bin.

When you think about it, how gross is that? Why would we want stinky trash just sitting in our kitchens? Trash is smelly. It's full of waste, moldy foods, and emptied products.

Interestingly, we struggle with taking out the trash in our own lives too. It's as if we get used to the stinky trash in our hearts. Instead of cleaning it up and taking it out, we push it down, adding more and more garbage to our souls. God is our parent with His hands on His hips, shaking His head, and telling us, "Your trash is stinking up this place. Take it out!"

We already know that we're fallen from grace. All of us are sinful, and our righteousness is "as filthy rags." But the blood of Christ cleanses us. Renewing our spirits cleans up our hearts. True repentance, daily repentance, is what's needed to "take out the trash."

Unfortunately, we get used to the trash. Sometimes we don't even see it or smell it in our lives. Our flesh is powerful. We wrestle with it daily. Paul says it's a war that goes on within himself. The Bible says that our flesh is enmity against God, which means that if we are going to walk in the will of God, we must die daily. Yes, in other words, we must take out the trash. Every. Single. Day.

What "trash" do we have in our lives? In Song of Solomon 2:15, we learn it's the little foxes that spoil the vines. If we're not careful, little things in our lives can ultimately destroy us.

We allow ourselves justification for wrong behaviors or thought-processes that do not help in moving us toward our visions or dreams. More so, these wrong behaviors and thought-processes can actually block the will of God from being fulfilled because we've become so accustomed to having these issues in our lives that we're unrepentant of them.

In my early twenties, I was not faithful in my tithe. I didn't even think about it. John always paid his, so I thought we were good. It's not as if God's keeping score, right? It wasn't until I attended a ladies' retreat, and the special speaker stirred my heart and convicted me. I had to repent of this failing. I'm not even sure what her title or main point was about. I only remember one sentence she said: "You're so busy begging God to bless you while you turn around and rob Him." Those words convicted and changed me. I'm glad to say I took out the trash that day and got right with the Lord.

If you want to know what "trash" you may have in your life, pray about it and ask God to reveal to you what areas in your life you need to work on. Trust me, God desires you to work on these issues. These "little foxes" could be hindering true spiritual growth. Once you are at a right place spiritually, ask someone (like a spouse or significant other or maybe even your pastor or spiritual leader) who is spirit-filled and who you trust to be honest with you to discuss what areas in your life he or she thinks you should work on. Do not become defensive or try to argue or explain yourself. Truly listen with an open mind and open heart. Remember, this is how others perceive you.

Another activity that is helpful and is a bit more introspective is to ask yourself this question: If I were a fly on the wall and could hear others complain about me, what would be their complaints? **Would they complain:**

- He/She is never on time!
- He/She is continually bossing us around!
- He/She has an anger problem! One wrong word, and he/she could go off.
- He/She struggles to communicate effectively! We never know what we're doing or what's going on because he/she doesn't tell us.
- He/She starts something and never finishes!
- He/She never really listens to what we have to say!
- He/She needs to be the center of attention! It's all about him/her!
- He/She struggles with lying. We never know if what he/she is saying is the truth!
- He/She can be really mean to people! If you're not in his/her circle of friends, he/she wants nothing to do with you.

Expect Greater

This list is in no way a comprehensive list, but it's some examples to get us thinking about others' perceptions of us. These areas could be the "trash" that is cluttering up our lives. It's difficult to grow in God when we have this kind of clutter taking up space in our hearts. That's because all of these examples are manifestations of unrepentant sins. Yes, that's right. Constant tardiness is a manifestation of other, more serious issues. Think about it: Pride, selfishness, vanity, deceitfulness, favoritism, are all areas that we would agree should not be in a Christian's life, yet each of the above complaints are manifestations of those sins.

Look at it this way (and warning, this may step on some toes):

- It is *selfish* to have others wait for you to get started, especially if you are habitually tardy. Why is others' time less valuable than yours?
- It is *arrogance* to consider your ideas and opinions more highly than others. Why must others do things your way?
- Losing your cool or being routinely volatile and/or emotional is *a lack of self-control*. Why subject others to your unchecked mood swings or temper flare-ups?
- A lack of communication is *frustrating to others* and can result in incomplete projects or dysfunctional endeavors. Don't be the cause or reason someone else stumbles!
- The need for attention is *selfish <u>and</u> arrogant*. Are others' talents and gifts any less than yours? If they're not of the same caliber as you, should not they not be given opportunities to learn how to improve and

develop in their callings?
- One lie leads to *broken trust*. This includes saying you're going to do something, and then not doing it.
- Meanness is *not the love of Christ*. If our actions and/or words cause others to feel badly about themselves, then we have fallen short of Christ's command to "love our neighbors as we love ourselves."

Galatians 5:9 explains "A little leaven leaveneth the whole lump." It doesn't take much to create major obstacles in our walks with God and in fulfilling His plan for our lives.

Secret Trash versus Acceptable Trash

There are two types of trash in our lives: the secret kind and the acceptable kind (and the word *acceptable* is being used loosely). The secret kinds of trash are the things and habits we do in secret. We don't want others to know that we struggle with pornography or raunchy books. We don't want others to find out that we struggle with covetousness. We know these things to be sinful. We may even repent often, only to fall back into the temptation. The Bible makes it clear that what we do in secret is open before the Lord. In Luke 12:2, Jesus states this: "For there is nothing covered, that shall not be revealed; neither hid, that shall not be known."

We are deceiving ourselves by thinking that what we do in secret will stay there. The One who matters most sees and knows everything, and I mean *everything*.
- "O God, thou knowest my foolishness; and my sins are not hid from thee," (Psalm 69:5).
- "Thou hast set our iniquities before thee, our secret

sins in the light of thy countenance," (Psalm 90:8).
- "For mine eyes are upon all their ways: they are not hid from my face, neither is their iniquity hid from mine eyes," (Jeremiah 16:17).

Not only does God see what we do and think in secret, but our thoughts and actions determine the trajectory of our lives. Simply put, we will not get away with it. "Be not deceived; God is not mocked: for whatsoever a man soweth, that shall he also reap," (Galatians 6:7).

I realize we live in a time where we want to feel comforted by the church. We want to hear that God is love. Leave that judgement and punishment stuff alone. That is not the whole truth. We have to talk about it, not only because our hearts are in desperate need of cleansing, but also because living in sin blocks God's plan for our lives.
- "And first I will recompense their iniquity and their sin double; because they have defiled my land, they have filled mine inheritance with the carcases of their detestable and abominable things," (Jeremiah 16:18).
- "He that covereth his sins shall not prosper: but whoso confesseth and forsaketh them shall have mercy," (Proverbs 28:13).

Then there is *acceptable* trash. It's the trash in our lives that we don't even bother to hide. It's the idols we have out in the open. More and more, as sin becomes acceptable, the list of acceptable trash is growing. There are those on the platforms of our churches living out of alignment of Scripture, yet we turn a blind eye because we don't want to cause offense.
- We gossip and criticize others without any thought to

the displeasure it brings the Lord.
- We turn our noses up at those with addictions, while our sugar and food addictions kill us. Smoking is not acceptable in church circles, yet gluttony is.
- We preach against fornication, yet promote selfies on social media to garner likes and attention.
- We scoff at Hollywood and the hedonistic culture, while idolizing ministers and musicians, placing them on pedestals meant only for God. They've become our golden calves for all to see.
- Even the love of money, which the Bible warns is "the root of all evil," has become acceptable in our lives, as we look to multi-million-dollar preachers and expansive venues for our religious direction.

Whether the trash of our lives is done in secret or out in the open, *it's still trash*. Don't allow it to clutter up your heart. God's will and purpose can be blocked or paused when we allow too much trash to collect in our lives. Just ask Samson.

Samson's Trouble

> *...When [Delilah] pressed him daily with her words, and urged him...*
> *That he told her all his heart, and said unto her, There hath not come a razor upon mine head; for I have been a Nazarite unto God from my mother's womb: if I be shaven, then my strength will go from me, and I shall*

Expect Greater

> *become weak, and be like any other man...*
> *And she made him sleep upon her knees; and she called for a man, and she caused him to shave off the seven locks of his head; and she began to afflict him, and his strength went from him.*
> *And she said, The Philistines be upon thee, Samson. And he awoke out of his sleep, and said, I will go out as at other times before, and shake myself. And he wist not that the Lord was departed from him.*
> *But the Philistines took him, and put out his eyes, and brought him down to Gaza, and bound him with fetters of brass; and he did grind in the prison house.*
> *Judges 16:16-17, 19-21*

Most of us know parts of Samson's story. He had amazing strength, got tricked by Delilah, and paid the ultimate price. But Samson had a lot of trash built up in his heart long before he ever met Delilah.

Samson lived as a judge for Israel, participating in the Nazarite vow of consecration and separation. God took this vow seriously. Some of the God-ordained guidelines meant that Samson couldn't drink wine or even eat grapes or raisins, he couldn't touch any dead thing, and he couldn't bring a razor to his head.

God's hand was on Samson, and Samson was known throughout the land for his amazing strength and incredible feats. One of his victories came at a small indiscretion. He slaughtered a thousand Philistines with the jawbone of a donkey. He was successful, but he had also made himself unclean by touching a dead thing (the jawbone). He also flirted with ungodly women, and even ordered his parents to get the girl he wanted when it went against their customs. These little offenses by themselves were probably no big deal to Samson, especially because his power and authority hadn't diminished.

Maybe that's why he eventually told Delilah his Nazarite secret. He wasn't a stupid man. She had already beguiled and betrayed him by sending the Philistines upon him. It's as if it was a game to Samson. He knew he was powerful. He knew the Philistines didn't stand a chance, but God was done playing games.

Samson knew his covenant was special, but he had collected too much unrepentant trash. He became complacent with the covenant, and it brought about his captivity and demise. Sometimes we do get away with the trash in our lives, at least at first. Samson had broken his Nazarite vow long before he whispered his secrets to Delilah.

A couple things in the trash are no big deal, or so it seems, but the challenge is that God and sin don't mix. An unrepentant heart, even over a little trash, will eventually wreak havoc in our lives. If we want God to freely move and lead us on the path of righteousness, every little piece of trash must be removed from our hearts. Sin is sin. God wants great things for us, but sin blocks that path.

Throw Out that Trash

The beauty of Samson's story is it shows that with true repentance, God can align us to His will once again. Samson was tortured—they gouged his eyes, shaved his head, used

Expect Greater

double the chains and kept him captive grinding grain at the mill—yet God forgave him and showed mercy when Samson asked. God's mercy led to the Philistines' defeat.

> *And it came to pass, when their hearts were merry, that they said, Call for Samson, that he may make us sport. And they called for Samson out of the prison house; and he made them sport: and they set him between the pillars. And Samson said unto the lad that held him by the hand, Suffer me that I may feel the pillars whereupon the house standeth, that I may lean upon them.*
>
> *Now the house was full of men and women; and all the lords of the Philistines were there; and there were upon the roof about three thousand men and women, that beheld while Samson made sport.*
>
> *And Samson called unto the Lord, and said, O Lord God, remember me, I pray thee, and strengthen me, I pray thee, only this once, O God, that I may be at once avenged of the Philistines for my two eyes.*
>
> *And Samson took hold of the two middle pillars upon which the house stood, and on which it was borne up, of the one with his right hand, and of the other with his left.*
>
> *And Samson said, Let me die with the Philistines. And he bowed himself with all his might; and the house fell upon the lords,*

*and upon all the people that were therein.
So the dead which he slew at his death were
more than they which he slew in his life.
Judges 16:25-30*

Maybe as you're reading this, you recognize areas of your life that you've held onto for too long. Whatever the situation you find yourself in, God's mercy never fails, but we have to take the trash that has collected in our lives and lay it at the foot of the cross. When we receive Christ's Spirit inside of us, not only are our hearts cleansed, but they are filled with the pure truth of the Holy Ghost. Think of the most pristine lake in the middle of a mountainous forest. A lake so pure that you can see straight through to the bottom. Now imagine garbage trucks plowing through the forest and dumping garbage into that pristine lake. One truckload, then another, then another. That is exactly what it's like when we allow unrepented sin into our lives and leave it to collect. It just doesn't belong.

Paul writes in Romans, "What shall we say then? Shall we continue in sin, that grace may abound? God forbid. How shall we, that are dead to sin, live any longer therein?" (Romans 6:1-2). We should never feel that we are too good for repentance, so take the time to pray. Ask God to reveal your sins, to reveal the areas of your life that need to be remedied, and watch how God begins to freely work in your life again.

Final Thoughts

In order to pursue God and experience His greater expectations, we need to take out the trash daily. Many believers expect blessings and favor that expressly go against God's will. This will only lead us further away from His purpose for us. Cast aside *anything* that goes against His Word.

The dumpster's calling. It's time to take out that trash.

Godly Pursuit #4: Trust Him

"Do you trust me?"

Well, that's a loaded question, isn't it?

Whenever I'm asked this question, I hesitate in my response, mostly because my truthful answer would be something along the lines of "No, not really."

We've already discussed my issues with control and letting go, but I would be remiss if I didn't outline this necessary step in pursuing God's plan and purpose for our lives. It ultimately comes down to *trust*.

Many of us have trust issues. The reasons are multi-faceted. We could struggle with trust because we have been hurt in our past. When enough people break your heart or betray your confidence, it's hard to trust others. I've found that trust issues often began when we were let down by someone.

What do trust issues look like? How do they manifest in our lives?

- We may struggle with control issues.
- We may doubt others' motives.
- We may be overwhelmed by the enormous responsibilities we've placed in our laps due to an unwillingness to delegate.

- We may be bitter with others who don't seem to care as much as we do about a specific project or situation.
- We complain that no one helps, while not allowing others to contribute in their own ways.
- We project our trust issues onto others.
- We manipulate to try to control the situation, which ultimately pushes others away.

Understanding this about ourselves is crucial when it comes to growing in our relationship with God, but trusting in God is monumental as we walk in His plan. As we've seen from previous chapters, God can take His sweet time when it comes to fulfilling His purpose. Think of everything David endured as he waited year after year for God's promise to be fulfilled. He didn't even have a home to lay his head! He ended up fighting alongside Israel's enemies because he was not wanted in his own land. Even through those trials, he is the one who penned, "Wait on the Lord: be of good courage, and he shall strengthen thine heart: wait, I say, on the Lord," (Psalm 27:14).

Look back over your life. Remember all the times God brought you through. Let that be a reminder that He is worthy of our trust. Jesus, while on earth, made a point to earn our trust. He did not leave us comfortless, and His promises still hold true today:

- **He promised to never leave us.**
    "…And, lo, I am with you always, even unto the end

of the world," (Matthew 28:20).

- **He promised to bear our burdens.**

"Come unto me, all ye that labour and are heavy laden, and I will give you rest. Take my yoke upon you, and learn of me; for I am meek and lowly in heart: and ye shall find rest unto your souls. For my yoke is easy, and my burden is light," (Matthew 11:28-30).

- **He promised to answer our prayers according to His will.**

"But seek ye first the kingdom of God, and his righteousness; and all these things shall be added unto you," (Matthew 6:33).

- **He promised to work things out for the good.**

"Therefore I say unto you, Take no thought for your life, what ye shall eat, or what ye shall drink; nor yet for your body, what ye shall put on. Is not the life more than meat, and the body than raiment? Behold the fowls of the air: for they sow not, neither do they reap, nor gather into barns; yet your heavenly Father feedeth them. Are ye not much better than they?" (Matthew 6:25-26).

"If ye then, being evil, know how to give good gifts unto your children: how much more shall your heavenly Father give the Holy Spirit to them that ask him?" (Luke 11:13).

- **He promised protection.**

"And I give unto them eternal life; and they shall never perish, neither shall any man pluck them out of my hand. My Father, which gave them me, is greater than all; and no man is able to pluck them out of my

Father's hand," (John 10:28-29).
- **He promised salvation.**
"For God so loved the world, that he gave his only begotten Son, that whosoever believeth in him should not perish, but have everlasting life. For God sent not his Son into the world to condemn the world; but that the world through him might be saved," (John 3:16-17).
- **He promised to come back again to us.**
"Let not your heart be troubled: ye believe in God, believe also in me. In my Father's house are many mansions: if it were not so, I would have told you. I go to prepare a place for you. And if I go and prepare a place for you, I will come again, and receive you unto myself; that where I am, there ye may be also," (John 14:1-3).

His promises are sure, but if we're not careful, we'll doubt him. Others have let us down, and we often judge our current circumstances based on past events. But "God is not man that he should lie," (Numbers 23:19). We need to be careful to not use others' failings as a measuring stick for God. His promises are yea and amen (2 Corinthians 1:20). Isaiah 55:11 shows that when God says it, it is going to happen: "So shall my word be that goeth forth out of my mouth: ***it shall not return unto me void***, but it shall accomplish that which I please, and it shall prosper in the thing whereto I sent it" [emphasis mine]. Let's give God the credit that's due Him.

Simply stated, He hasn't failed us yet. We can rest assured that He's not about to start.

Daniel's Lesson in Trust

> Then the king commanded, and they brought Daniel, and cast him into the den of lions. Now the king spake and said unto Daniel, Thy God whom thou servest continually, he will deliver thee...
>
> Then the king went to his palace, and passed the night fasting: neither were instruments of musick brought before him: and his sleep went from him.
>
> Then the king arose very early in the morning, and went in haste unto the den of lions... he cried with a lamentable voice unto Daniel: and the king spake and said to Daniel, O Daniel, servant of the living God, is thy God, whom thou servest continually, able to deliver thee from the lions?
>
> Then said Daniel unto the king, O king, live for ever. My God hath sent his angel, and hath shut the lions' mouths, that they have not hurt me: forasmuch as before him innocency was found in me; and also before thee, O king, have I done no hurt.
>
> Daniel 6:16, 18-22

Daniel faced the ultimate test: imminent death. Much like Joseph, Daniel did not deserve the punishment. The king's men were jealous of Daniel's favor with the king and set out to destroy him any way they could. Since Daniel was honorable, the only way to destroy him was to attack his religious practices. By tricking King Darius into making a law prohibiting any form of prayer or worship to anyone or anything other than the king, these jealous men sealed Daniel's fate. From Daniel's point of view, imagine how frightening the situation: Give up his daily prayer or face death. If it were me, I'd be questioning God while they dragged me to the lion's den. The Bible makes no mention of Daniel's state of mind. On the contrary, the Bible speaks specifically of the king's anxiety over the situation.

God had it all under control just like He always does. Daniel continued in favor with the king while the jealous men were thrown in the lions' den and devoured.

Trust Him in the Process

The process to get to where we're going is troublesome. God's power was revealed to the king and to his advisors when Daniel came from the den unscathed, yet Daniel still had to go through God's plan to get to that other side. He had to endure the darkness in a den full of hungry lions. Some of us have had to endure metaphoric darkness in a den full of hungry lions, and how did we respond?

Daniel had to trust that God knew what He was doing. For a while, it didn't look so good. Those who were against him seemed powerful and had the ear of the king. They rose up against him, and it appeared that their corruption would not only win but would jeopardize Daniel's life.

Daniel's contemporaries—Shadrach, Meshach, and Abednego—were three Hebrew young men who also lived in Babylon and served in the king's court. The king was King Nebuchadnezzar, and he had erected a 90-foot statue of himself. His expectation was that everyone would bow and worship the statue. When the three Hebrew young men refused to bow, they had to endure a process that no doubt brought questions. Trusting God is easy to say, but when the soldiers are making the furnace so hot that they were dying, it was probably difficult to keep the faith that God had a handle on the situation. But He did. God delivered them from the fiery furnace and showed King Nebuchadnezzar who the real King of Kings was, is, and will forever be.

> *He answered and said, Lo, I see four men loose, walking in the midst of the fire, and they have no hurt; and the form of the fourth is like the Son of God. Daniel 3:25*

The process did not affect these men's faith or trust in God. Daniel wasn't about to stop praying, and Shadrach, Meshach, and Abednego weren't about to worship anything or anyone other than the one true God. Our day-to-day walk with the Lord is a process that, if we let it, will bring us closer to Him. The process is going to place us in situations where we have to trust God. But truly trusting Him leads us into walking out His will and unleashing His power in our lives. Divine power and million-dollar bank accounts are not often synonymous, but divine power unleashes the supernatural in our lives. And it changes lives. Just like it did for Daniel. Just like it did for Shadrach, Meshach, and Abednego.

The Process has a Purpose

The Gospel's account of the Garden of Gethsemane is heart

Expect Greater

wrenching. Jesus knew what had to happen. Jesus understood His purpose on earth, and yet our Savior knelt in the garden, praying so fervently that His body reacted by sweating large drops that historians say could very well have been blood.

> *And being in an agony he prayed more earnestly: and his sweat was as it were great drops of blood falling down to the ground.*
> Luke 22:44

Jesus faced death, and He *knew* it. He *knew* the hearts of those who accused Him, and He did it anyway. He *knew* that Peter—one of His closest friends—would betray Him, and He did it anyway. He *knew* that the disciples would scatter, leaving Him alone in His torment, but He did it anyway. In that moment, in the Garden of Gethsemane, we see Jesus's ultimate submission and complete humility to the perfect will of God. In this moment, it should show all of us that even Jesus had to grapple with God's purpose and the process He would have to endure to have that purpose fulfilled.

The process is never easy because it entails dying to our flesh and truly submitting to God. The process involves questions and often perceived loneliness. It often involves tears and frustration. But it's not supposed to be easy. Remember, we are fallen men and women under the curse of Adam. God's process must be a refining fire.

> *But who may abide the day of his coming?*

> *and who shall stand when he appeareth? for he is like a refiner's fire, and like fullers' soap:*
> *Malachi 3:2*

In order for His plan and purpose to be fulfilled in our lives, He must prepare us. We may come as we are to Jesus, but we should never stay as we are. A true covenant with our Creator must involve complete repentance and submission.

Not our will, His.

Not our desires, His.

Not our flesh, but His Spirit.

That's why being infilled with the Holy Spirit is a necessity. We need His power to endure His process.

With this understanding, we too can say as Jesus said, "…Nevertheless, not my will, but thine, be done," (Luke 22:42).

Final Thoughts

Even when we are doing everything right, it is hard to trust God in the midst of the storm. Daniel's experience in the lion's den and the three Hebrew young men's experience in the fiery furnace show us how God's power was able to be seen throughout the land. The process, however, was not easy. These men's lives were in jeopardy because of their faith. The lions *should* have killed Daniel. The fiery furnace *should* have killed the three Hebrew young men. We know—because we're on the other side of these stories—that God came through and protected them, but can you imagine going through it? How many of us would have caved into pressure as they're dragging us to the lion's den or to the raging fire?

And then there's Jesus, who lost His life (temporarily), and not only that, but it was God's will for Him to lose His life for the redemption of all mankind.

These examples show God's purpose has a process, and it is not easy. However, God will *never* leave us without peace and His presence. Ultimately, even when we don't understand the *how* or *why* of a situation, trusting that God's will is for our good will bring us into alignment with His plan.

Let it be so, Lord Jesus. Let it be so.

Godly Pursuit #5: Truly Submit

Submission is a four-letter word to those with a worldly mindset. Our society flaunts its independence. Companies can't keep workers because people simply get annoyed or don't like being told what to do, so they walk off the jobs. As an educator, I've been dismayed with young people's lack of respect to those in authority. I've been yelled at, cursed at, and threatened by students *and* their parents.

Some may argue that submitting to someone lets that person have power over you. Power can get to someone's head, which might lead to mistreatment. In the wrong hands, yes, I can see this point. In the 19th century, Lord Acton is credited for saying, "Absolute power corrupts absolutely." I too have unfortunately been on the other end of this power struggle where those in authority over me have mistreated me and abused their power.

Isn't it interesting that God requires true submission? He doesn't just require a little bit of submission here and there, but He requires complete submission of the heart, mind, body, and soul. If we want to walk in the will of the Lord, humbling ourselves before Him and trusting His guidance are paramount.

The Paradox of Submission

The story of Creation reveals the nature of God. He's an artist, while at the same time creating harmony and balance for sustenance and aesthetic value. It's a marvel. His greatest creation—mankind—was given a certain amount of power in the form of free will.

> *And God said, Let us make man in our image, after our likeness: and let them have dominion over the fish of the sea, and over the fowl of the air, and over the cattle, and over all the earth, and over every creeping thing that creepeth upon the earth.*
> *Genesis 1:26*

This God-given authority is powerful because ultimately, we choose our paths. God may have a plan for us, but it's our decision whether or not we'll submit to it. Therin lies the paradox. We're given the power—or authority—over our lives... *to submit.*

What?

So, we're given power only to hand it back?

The power is the choice. Submission means admitting that although we have the choice, we can't do it without God's intervention. Interestingly, when we make the decision to humble ourselves before the Lord and submit to His authority, we receive power even greater than our own.

- "O that thou hadst hearkened to my commandments! then had thy peace been as a river, and thy

righteousness as the waves of the sea" Isaiah 48:18.
- "But ye shall receive power, after that the Holy Ghost is come upon you..." (Acts 1:8).
- "...I have set before you life and death, blessing and cursing: therefore *choose* life, that both thou and thy seed may live: That thou mayest love the Lord thy God, and that thou mayest obey his voice, and that thou mayest cleave unto him: for he is thy life, and the length of thy days: that thou mayest dwell in the land which the Lord sware unto thy fathers, to Abraham, to Isaac, and to Jacob, to give them," (Deuteronomy 30:19-20).

The fact is that our "power"—if we want to call it that—is severely limited. For example, we live in the present and can remember the past, but we can't change it. We can also hope for the future and envision the future, but we do not know what's going to happen. We are confined to time, and that places a limit on our authority. Our power over others is also severely limited because they, like us, have free will and can choose to not listen to us or to do as we say. Many of us—if we're being completely honest—would admit that often we feel powerless.

God is *all* powerful. He holds the universe in His hands. He exists outside of time and the parameters set by it through His creative hand. He's not confined to the present. He knows that if you trust Him and submit to His authority, the trajectory of your life will be guided by the best, most capable hands. *His.*

The Rich Young Ruler

We don't know a lot about the rich young ruler, other than he had a place of prominence in society, lived a prosperous life, and was already following the ten commandments. He was basically doing everything he was supposed to be doing…or so he thought.

> *Jesus said unto him, If thou wilt be perfect, go and sell that thou hast, and give to the poor, and thou shalt have treasure in heaven: and come and follow me. But when the young man heard that saying, he went away sorrowful: for he had great possessions.*
> *Then said Jesus unto his disciples, Verily I say unto you, That a rich man shall hardly enter into the kingdom of heaven.*
> *And again I say unto you, It is easier for a camel to go through the eye of a needle, than for a rich man to enter into the kingdom of God.*
> Matthew 19:21-24

Ultimately, it came down to whether or not the rich young ruler would submit to what Jesus was calling him to do. God knows what has a hold on our hearts. That's exactly what He'll zero in on for us to let go.

The rich young ruler's situation is similar to ours because many of us live in prosperity and comfort. Even in our struggles, we are blessed with so much. Yet how many of us struggle to faithfully give our tithe and offerings? How many of us struggle to give of our time in ministries? How many of us focus on our own problems and our own families that we don't make room for truly being the kingdom of God in our communities? Our prosperity has made us comfortable to the point that when Jesus calls us—and He *is* calling us—we question the calling, especially when it means giving up our comfort.

When ministering, I often ask the question, "If I were to ask your work/school if you are truly a Christian, what would be the response?" If the answer is that they wouldn't know that you were even a Christian, that's a problem…and a wake-up call. Equally convicting would be a response along the lines of, "Well, he says he's a Christian, but if that's Christianity, I want nothing to do with it." This was the hypocrisy of the Pharisees. The religious leaders of Jesus' day dressed the part and often acted important, but Jesus saw through them: "Woe unto you, scribes and Pharisees, hypocrites! for ye are like unto whited sepulchres, which indeed appear beautiful outward, but are within full of dead men's bones, and of all uncleanness," (Matthew 23:27).

What does this have to do with submission? True submission to God's authority is *noticeable*. Jesus says as much:

Ye are the salt of the earth: but if the salt have lost his savour, wherewith shall it be salted? it is thenceforth good for nothing, but to be cast out, and to be trodden under

> *foot of men.*
> *Ye are the light of the world. A city that is set on an hill cannot be hid.*
> *Neither do men light a candle, and put it under a bushel, but on a candlestick; and it giveth light unto all that are in the house.*
> *Let your light so shine before men, that they may see your good works, and glorify your Father which is in heaven.*
> *Matthew 5: 13-16*

Truly submitting to God is understanding that His will is for all to seek Him and repent. Every single day, we are the walking, talking miracles of the goodness of the Lord. Submitting to Him allows that testimony to shine. However, if we are not truly submitted, if we do not give up our comforts and complacency, then are we truly followers of Christ? Are we like the rich young ruler who knew the commandments and feel like he was serving the Lord, when really, if we stood before Jesus, we would walk away from Him hanging our heads in shame?

As discussed in the previous chapter, Daniel and three Hebrew young men submitted themselves to God's will, even to the point of death. Some of us can't even submit ourselves to the cause of Christ to be faithful in church attendance, let alone to volunteer time and resources to feed the poor, visit the sick, or minister to those in prisons.

Naaman and the Jordan River

> *So Naaman came with his horses and with his chariot, and stood at the door of the house of Elisha.*
> *And Elisha sent a messenger unto him, saying, "Go and wash in the Jordan seven times, and thy flesh shall come again to thee, and thou shalt be clean."*
> *But Naaman was wroth, and went away, and said, "Behold, I thought, He will surely come out to me and stand, and call on the name of the Lord his God, and strike his hand over the place and recover the leper. Are not Abana and Pharpar, rivers of Damascus, better than all the waters of Israel? May I not wash in them, and be cleansed?"*
> *So he turned and went away in a rage.*
> *II Kings 5:9-12*

There's been a time or two when I've been annoyed and even a little angry over what God wanted me to do. I've said, "That doesn't even make sense!" several times in my prayer life. I understand Naaman's frustration. This man is used to having things his way, yet he's stricken with a horrible, debilitating disease. He gathers up enough gumption to go to Elisha the prophet in the first place. Elisha doesn't even greet him. Instead, a messenger tells him to go and dip seven times in the Jordan river. That response took Naaman by surprise. It wasn't what he expected. The command didn't make any sense, and it made Naaman angry. The Bible states that he "went off in a rage."

It's at this point that most of us come to a crossroads, just like Naaman. We have a decision to make. Trust in the Lord and follow His will—even if it makes no sense—or do it our way? If Naaman would have done it his way, he would have died a horrific death as a leper. Instead, he swallowed his pride, realized he had nothing to lose, and dipped himself seven times in the Jordan. He humbled himself and submitted wholly to the plan of God.

Will you? Will you forsake your idols, your complacency, your will, and follow Jesus? Even if it means forsaking your desires, handing them to Jesus, and taking up the cross? The paradox of submission is that truly submitting to God's plan will open the doors to His provision and favor. Greater things come when this important step happens.

Final Thoughts

When we start trusting in God and start believing that His expectations are greater than our own, the crux of it all depends upon our submission. Dying to our will and desires so that God's will can be revealed in our lives is not easy. God, however, honors obedience. When we submit to the Lord, we will find great freedom and power in Him and through Him.

Godly Pursuit #6: Work Hard

My first real job was the Chicken Shack. I ran the counter and register and made $3.50 an hour. I actually turned fourteen the week I began the job. I babysat for a couple years before the Chicken Shack, but this was the first job I received a paycheck with taxes taken out.

I've been working ever since.

In high school, I held an array of jobs: ½ Off Card Shop, Babies 'R Us, A & W Root Beer, and 7-11. My parents made it clear if I wanted a car and some freedom, then I needed a j-o-b. This never bothered me. I liked working. There's a certain satisfaction that comes from earning a paycheck. I could go out to eat with my friends without asking my parents for money. (They would have said "no" anyway.) I could buy my own clothes and accessories.

Back then, my parents taught me to take my job seriously. The idea of "calling in" mortified my parents, so I was taught to show up on time and ready to work. That mentality has never left me.

When Jonathan—my now 22-year-old—first began working, my husband and I taught him the same work ethic. Don't call in. Be reliable and responsible. Don't show up late. Be respectful to management, employees, and customers no matter what. My son took that advice to heart. His work ethic got him through college with a learning disability. His work ethic impressed the undersheriff of a local county, landing him a prime internship in criminal justice. With a degree in hand, he walked right into an excellent position at another sheriff's department, where he's worked for over a year and earns almost as much as I do!

What do these examples have to do with expecting greater?

Part of God's expectations for our lives is for us to work, and not only to work, but to work hard. We have to have some skin in the game, so to speak. I've never heard of God's promises falling into someone's lap without any effort. Sure, it might seem like the Jones' have everything they want, and they have easy lives, but let's get the beam out of our own eye, roll up our sleeves, and get to work.

Why? Because God *expects* it.

Spiritual Work versus Physical Labor

We are flesh and spirit. Both require work to align ourselves to the will of God. Spiritual work involves pursuing Godliness and intimacy with Him. Prayer and fasting are two necessary components to getting our spiritual selves in shape. Isaiah 55:6 says, "Seek ye the LORD while he may be found…" and Matthew 6:33 reminds us, "Seek ye first the kingdom of God…" Seeking God is spiritual work. We're naturally of the flesh, so we have to purposefully set aside our flesh to pursue a relationship with Christ.

Physical labor is also important to the Lord. We have dominion in this world, and that means that we must work to cultivate it. We must cultivate land, our dwellings, and the many systems that lead to us living prosperous lives. None of this can happen without work. Moreover, God uses our physical labor to reach others and bless them. This can't happen if we're camping out in our homes watching game shows and soap operas. This is not to say that working at home in the raising of families doesn't constitute as work. Any parent knows that it is hard work raising children and taking care of their families. However, God does not tolerate laziness, and the Bible highlights several examples of this.

At times, our spiritual and physical work are out of balance. We may take our prayer life seriously, yet we struggle to keep a job. Or, we may have a strong work ethic, yet our spiritual selves are lacking. We've examined several spiritual expectations in fulfilling God's plan, but several Biblical examples illustrate that God's plan materialized during physical labor.

Cast the Nets

Several of Jesus' disciples were fishermen. This can be a treacherous job and is wholly reliant on factors outside of their control. This example shows that the disciples were diligently working, even when nothing was going their way. It was because they were in their boats working, Jesus was able to provide for them an overabundance of what they sought after.

> ...*He said unto Simon, Launch out into the deep, and let down your nets for a draught. And Simon answering said unto him, Master, we have toiled all the night, and have taken nothing: nevertheless at thy word I will let down the net. And when they had this done, they inclosed a great*

multitude of fishes: and their net brake.
Luke 5:4-6

I find the word Simon used interesting: *toiled*. Toil means to work hard to the point of physical exhaustion. The miracle happened while they worked. The night had not gone well for them. They had yet to catch a single fish. How draining that must have been to cast, then recast the nets, only to produce nothing, yet Simon needed to be right where he was for Jesus to step into the situation. Would this miracle have taken place if Simon had been on the shore?

Most of us can connect to Simon's predicament. We have toiled for weeks, months, years, and we can become tired and discouraged, but it's in our toil that Jesus makes a way out of no way. It's not in laziness or procrastination. We need to keep working, trusting, and casting our nets.

Planting? Watering? Or Harvesting?

Paul verifies this Godly principle in I Corinthians 3:6: "I have planted, Apollos watered; but God gave the increase." This verse doesn't say "…and some sat and waited for God to make it happen…"

Actually, Scripture refers to sowing seeds and planting several times in reference to kingdom work. Farming was integral in the infrastructure of that time period. If they didn't plant, there wouldn't be a harvest. When the harvest came, they'd have to glean the fields. Then the process started all over again.

That's where Ruth met Boaz. She was gleaning the field.

> *...Boaz commanded his young men, saying, Let her glean even among the sheaves, and reproach her not:*
> *And let fall also some of the handfuls of purpose for her, and leave them, that she may glean them, and rebuke her not.*
> *So she gleaned in the field until even, and beat out that she had gleaned: and it was about an ephah of barley.*
> *Ruth 2:15-17*

Ruth wasn't waiting for Boaz; she was in the field! He first spotted her while she *worked*. This story would be much different if she never showed up. If she decided to stay at home and wait for Boaz to come to her, she might have remained a widow. Instead, by being where she was supposed to be and working hard to provide for her and Naomi, she was blessed by God. She not only married Boaz, but Jesus himself descended from her lineage.

In the same way that Boaz noticed Ruth in the field, God watches us. He watches us show up. He watches us work. When we are diligent and industrious, He rewards us openly, just as Boaz did with Ruth. Boaz explained to Ruth, "The Lord recompense thy work, and a full reward be given thee of the Lord God of Israel...," (Ruth 2:12).

What is it that God is calling you to do? Once we have that word from God, it's time to get to work. Whether it be planting, watering, or harvesting, that word will only come to fruition when we push ourselves to press forward and get ourselves to the field to work. Trust that Jesus will do His part—He's never failed—and we need to make sure we're doing our part.

Each Body Part Works

Each of us have a part to play in God's perfect plan. Some of us may feel insignificant or that our role isn't as important as someone else's. The Bible, however, says differently:

> *For as the body is one, and hath many members, and all the members of that one body, being many, are one body: so also [is] Christ.*
> *For by one Spirit are we all baptized into one body, whether [we be] Jews or Gentiles, whether [we be] bond or free; and have been all made to drink into one Spirit.*
> *For the body is not one member, but many.*
> *If the foot shall say, Because I am not the hand, I am not of the body; is it therefore not of the body?*
> *And if the ear shall say, Because I am not the eye, I am not of the body; is it therefore not of the body?*
> *If the whole body [were] an eye, where [were] the hearing? If the whole [were] hearing, where [were] the smelling?*
> *But now hath God set the members every one of them in the body, as it hath pleased him.*
> *I Corinthians 12:12-18*

If we consider our bodies, we are complex, inter-structural beings. Last week, Jonathan, my oldest son, moved into his own home. I was helping him paint a bedroom, and the next morning, I had muscles hurting all over my body. I joked, "I have muscles hurting that I didn't know existed!" All of these muscles were needed while painting. If you've ever broken, fractured, or sprained some part of your body, then you realize how important that part of your body is in everyday function.

Ever pull your back out? You'll be in bed for days.

Ever twist your ankle? You won't be able to walk right for weeks.

In my early twenties, I tripped outside a grocery store and sprained an ankle and injured both of my knees. It wasn't until I tried sitting and standing back up that I realized how integral knees were for completing the necessary movement! All these examples demonstrate the importance of all our body parts. Our bodies are balanced and aligned when everything is working together.

The Bible says that we are the body of Christ. There are many parts that make up that one body. God expects us to work together so that His body is not dysfunctional, but how can we work together when some of us have yet to start working? What would happen if the kidneys stopped working? Or the liver? Or the heart?

I'm waiting on the Lord.

Someone else will pick up the slack.

If we are not doing our part, then the body is not working to its full potential. When we don't do our part, according to God's design and purpose, there are definite ramifications.

The Curse of the Fig Tree

Consider Jesus' response to the fig tree that bore no fruit. It had a job to do. The expectation was that there would be figs to eat. When Jesus' expectation was not met, His response was swift.

> *And when [Jesus] saw a fig tree in the way, he came to it, and found nothing thereon, but leaves only, and said unto it, Let no fruit grow on thee henceforward for ever. And presently the fig tree withered away.*
> *And when the disciples saw it, they marvelled, saying, How soon is the fig tree withered away!*
> Matthew 21:19-20

Jesus expects our lives to bear fruit. This expectation cannot be met if we are not working on bearing fruit. Some may question Jesus' actions and may even wonder if the Lord acted rashly. Maybe the tree was a late bloomer. However, it came down to expectations, and everything Jesus did, as recorded in Scripture, had an important truth to it. Just as with the fig tree, God has expectations for our lives. Walking in alignment with His purpose and plan means that we will become more kingdom-minded, and our lives will bear spiritual fruit. When Jesus comes to our "fig trees," we need to be ready. So, whether we're watering, planting, or harvesting, when He examines us, let our hard work produce Godly fruit for the kingdom.

The cursed fig tree is only one example of tough love. The Bible contains more tough love when it comes to working. In 2 Thessalonians 3:10, Paul writes, "For even when we were with you, this we commanded you, that if any would not work, neither should he eat." In the book of Proverbs, it states, "How long wilt thou sleep, O sluggard? When wilt thou arise out of thy sleep? Yet a little sleep, a little slumber, a little folding of the hands to sleep: So shall thy poverty come as one that travelleth, and thy want as an armed man."

Final Thoughts

Aligning our desires with God's plan involves work. Please don't fool yourself into believing that there's nothing you need to be doing in order for God's plan to be fulfilled. God expects us to be doers. James reminded us of this: "But be ye doers of the word, and not hearers only, deceiving your own selves," (James 1:22). We already know God's going to do His part. We need to make sure that we're doing ours.

Godly Pursuit #7: Give Thanks

When was the last time you received a thank you card? My mom would write thank you cards all the time. There's something wonderful about receiving acknowledgment and appreciation for thoughtfulness.

I admit I'm the type of individual who becomes a little annoyed when someone doesn't say thank you when I hold the door open for them. If I let a driver in, and they don't acknowledge it somehow—like with a nod or a wave—I envision magically going back in time and not letting them pull in front of me. I know, I know, these are not the best traits to admit to, but in all honesty, I'd have a pretty long list of annoyances about ungrateful people. It's probably best that I don't make that list.

This doesn't mean I stop doing nice things or stop giving to others, but it does mean that sometimes I pause my giving when the gift-getter starts taking my generosity for granted. God has much more patience than I do, but the Bible describes a few times when even His patience ran out. "And when the people complained, it displeased the LORD: and the LORD heard it; and his anger was kindled; and the fire of the LORD burnt among them, and consumed them that were in the uttermost parts of the camp," (Numbers 11:1).

Expect Greater

Whereas complaining upsets God, our thanksgiving is a sweet-smelling sacrifice. In our pursuit of God, entering His presence with thanksgiving opens the doors for blessing and favor.

Ten Lepers, One Thankful Heart

> *And as he entered into a certain village, there met him ten men that were lepers, which stood afar off:*
> *And they lifted up their voices, and said, Jesus, Master, have mercy on us.*
> *And when he saw them, he said unto them, Go shew yourselves unto the priests. And it came to pass, that, as they went, they were cleansed.*
> *And one of them, when he saw that he was healed, turned back, and with a loud voice glorified God,*
> *And fell down on his face at his feet, giving him thanks: and he was a Samaritan.*
> *And Jesus answering said, Were there not ten cleansed? but where are the nine?*
> *There are not found that returned to give glory to God, save this stranger.*
> *And he said unto him, Arise, go thy way: thy faith hath made thee whole.*
> Luke 17:12-19

Jesus' compassion toward the ten lepers resulted in the

miraculous. All ten of them called out to Him and were healed. However, they were not whole. Luke's account makes a clear distinction between those who were healed and the one who became whole. Being healed means that the leprosy completely left their bodies. They were disease-free, but the disease of leprosy causes deformity. The effects of it are apparent. Being made whole means that not only was the disease gone, but there were no after effects of the disease. It also could mean spiritual and mental wholeness, as well as the physical aspect. What we do know is that the gratitude of the one brought him greater blessings and fulfillment.

When Jesus asked where the other nine lepers were, he already knew the answer. What He was doing was showing those around him that it did not escape his notice that only one came back.

Think of how you feel when someone gives you a genuine thank you. Think of how you feel when someone honors you publicly. It warms your heart. It makes you feel valued and appreciated. We are made in the image of our Creator, so how is He any different?

The Power of Thanksgiving

Two things here: Thankfulness requires action, and true thankfulness moves the very heart of God.

"There's always something to complain about," my mom said, "But complaining about it doesn't change anything." I saw the power of thanksgiving first-hand through my mother. She was a worshipper. She'd praise God in the car. She'd shout before service. She'd pray in the early hours of the mornings. And her prayers were always filled with thanksgiving.

"Thank you for your goodness," she'd say.
"Thank you for loving me."
"Thank you for my family."

The more she thanked God, the more intense her praise and worship became. The spirit would fall on her, and that was that. We kids would have to wait out the worship experience. Now that I'm an adult, I can pinpoint the power of thanksgiving that led to the favor and blessings of the Lord.

We can say we're thankful, but is our life a reflection of a thankful heart? Based off of Scripture, a thankful heart takes time out of their day to honor and worship God. Worship is more than just lip-service. It's honoring him with our lives, and following the Great Commission.

- A thankful heart cannot be bitter, cannot be negative, cannot be full of strife and conflict, cannot be full of manipulation and lies, and cannot be mean-spirited.
- A thankful heart realizes the blessings and favor of God and desires to bless others as they have been blessed.
- A thankful heart cannot be selfish but wants to give back.
- A thankful heart cannot be entitled or spoiled or arrogant. When the cleansed leper dropped at the feet of Jesus and worshiped him, he did so with a humble heart.
- When you are truly thankful and your life's action reflects that gratitude, it moves the very heart of God.

If we want God to start moving in our lives, we need to be thankful and practice it to those around us. Worship God in our thankfulness by being kind and going the extra mile. Worship God in our thankfulness by taking time every day to pray and reflect on His goodness. Worship God in our thankfulness by being the one who runs to Him only to fall at His feet in awe and humility.

Final Thoughts

If we want God's attention, we need to start with thanksgiving. Let it become a daily routine. Let words of gratitude come forth from our mouths and watch God move in our lives.

My Letter to You...

Dear Reader,

Life is hard. It seems we barely overcome one battle before another comes raging through. Sometimes in my own life, it feels I barely have my nose above the water. I feel as if I'm drowning and begging for a lifeline while my hopes and dreams of my future dim and fade as reality sets in. Trust me when I say I've been there. Many times. It's hard to have faith when the waves crash against your boat. It's hard to expect greater when you don't even know if you can make it past today.

But you can. I'm a living testimony of the goodness of God. I'm alive today, walking in the purpose of God because I chose faith over fear. I chose hope over anxiety. I chose trust over doubt. Sometimes, I must remind myself of these decisions. "No, Janice, you are not going to give into fear… No, Janice, let the anger go… Take a deep breath, Janice, God brought you out before, He'll do it again."

It makes sense for us to have expectations of God. Psalm 62:5 says, "My soul, wait thou only upon God; for my expectation is from him." Yet expecting greater is not about expecting amazing, wonderful gifts from the Lord, as much as it's about understanding that God expects greater for our lives than we could ever imagine. When we align ourselves and our desires with His will, we can and should expect greater.

I'm believing in greater things for each of our lives, most importantly a greater relationship with Jesus than we ever thought possible. It is only through Him and by Him that we will fulfill our God-given purpose and complete the plans He has set out for us.

Sincerely,
Janice Broyles

Janice Broyles

Thank you for your purchase!

Please visit ***www.janicebroyles.com*** for more about the author and her published work, including:

No Longer Rejected:
A Woman's Journey from Rejection to Freedom

www.ingramcontent.com/pod-product-compliance
Lightning Source LLC
Chambersburg PA
CBHW072005070526
44583CB00015B/1346